Oracle SQL
A Beginner's Tutorial

Second Edition

Djoni Darmawikarta

Oracle SQL, A Beginner's Tutorial, Second Edition
Copyright © 2016 by Brainy Software Inc.
Cover image © Dollar Photo Club
Second Edition: February 2016

ISBN: 9781771970303

Book and Cover Designer: Brainy Software Team

Technical Reviewer: Budi Kurniawan

Trademarks
Oracle and Java are registered trademarks of Oracle and/or its affiliates.
UNIX is a registered trademark of The Open Group.
Microsoft Internet Explorer is either a registered trademark or a trademark of Microsoft Corporation in The United States and/or other countries.
Apache is a trademark of The Apache Software Foundation.
Firefox is a registered trademark of the Mozilla Foundation.
Google is a trademark of Google, Inc.

Throughout this book the printing of trademarked names without the trademark symbol is for editorial purpose only. We have no intention of infringement of the trademark.

Warning and Disclaimer
Every effort has been made to make this book as accurate as possible. The author and the publisher shall have neither liability nor responsibility to any person or entity with respect to any loss or damages arising from the information in this book.

About the Author

Djoni Darmawikarta specializes in database, data modeling, data warehousing, and data analysis. He is a former systems engineer, consultant, customer support manager, and country computing center head at IBM. Djoni is currently a senior data analyst at a Toronto-based insurance company.

Table of Contents

Introduction

Welcome to *Oracle SQL: A Tutorial, Second Edition*. This book is for you if you want to learn SQL the easy way. SQL, which stands for Structured Query Language and is pronounced es-cue-el, is the standard language you use to interact with a relational database management system (RDBMS). This book uses the free edition of the Oracle database to show how SQL works.

SQL Overview

Initially developed at IBM in the early 1970s, SQL was formalized by the American National Standards Institute (ANSI) in 1986. Since then the SQL standard has been revised seven times. The examples in this book were tested using Oracle database 11g Release 2, which conforms to the SQL:2008 standard. This standard is one revision earlier than SQL:2011, the latest standard.

SQL consists of a data definition language (DDL) and a data manipulation language (DML). The DDL is used to create, delete, and alter the structure of a table and other database objects. The DML is used to insert, retrieve, and update data in a table or tables.

Many database vendors implement a version of SQL that is not 100% compliant with the standard. They often add unique features to their SQL, resulting in a new SQL dialect. For example, the following are some of the differences between Oracle SQL and MySQL SQL.

- The **AS** reserved word in the CREATE TABLE AS INSERT statement is mandatory in Oracle SQL but optional in MySQL SQL
- The Oracle INSERT statement can only insert one row; the MySQL INSERT statement can insert multiple rows.
- Oracle SQL supports UNION, INTERSECT and MINUS set operators whereas MySQL only supports UNION.
- The Oracle PL/SQL equivalent in MySQL is the stored routine (MySQL did not give a name to its procedural language extension). PL/SQL has much more functions than the stored routine.

Because of these dialects, SQL statements written for one RDBMS may not necessarily work in other RDBMS's.

About This Book

This book consists of thirteen chapters and four appendixes. This section gives you an overview of each chapter and appendix.

Chapter 1, "Storing and Maintaining Data" starts the book by discussing how data is stored and maintained in a relational database. In this chapter you learn how to create and maintain tables, as well as use SQL INSERT, UPDATE, DELETE, and MERGE statements to manipulate data.

Chapter 2, "Basic Queries" explains how to construct queries using the SELECT statement.

Chapter 3, "Query Output" shows how you can format query outputs beyond simply displaying columns of data from a database.

Chapter 4, "Grouping" explains what a group is, how to create a group, and how to apply aggregate functions to a group.

Chapter 5, "Joins" talks about the JOIN clause for querying data from multiple tables.

Chapter 6, "Subqueries" discusses the subquery. A subquery is a query that can be nested in another query.

Chapter 7, "Compound Queries" talks about set operators for combining the outputs of multiple queries.

Chapter 8, "Views" discusses views, which are predefined queries that you create and store in a database.

Chapter 9, "Built-in Functions" discusses some of the most commonly used built-in functions in the Oracle database.

Chapter 10, "Regular Expressions" shows you how to use regular expressions in SQL queries.

Chapter 11, "PL/SQL" introduces the Oracle PL/SQL programming language. PL/SQL extends SQL and is used to create user-defined function and stored procedure You also use PL/SQL to create triggers.

Chapter 12, "Granting Permissions" talks about how you allow others to use the database objects you create.

Chapter 13, "The Data Dictionary" shows how to use the data dictionary, the metadata of a database, to find information about the database.

Appendix A, "Installing Oracle Database XE" is a guide to installing Oracle Database Express Edition and making preparations for trying out the book examples.

Appendix B, "Oracle Built-in Data Types" provides a list of Oracle built-in data types.

Appendix C, "Indexing" covers the various indexing techniques available in the Oracle database.

Finally, Appendix D, "Oracle SQL Developer" introduces Oracle SQL Developer, an integrated development environment (IDE) for every database developer. This appendix introduces some of the features of this free GUI tool.

Code Conventions

SQL is not case sensitive. In this book, however, SQL reserved words such as CREATE and SELECT and keywords such as COUNT and MAX are written in upper case. To find the complete SQL reserved words, please refer to the Oracle SQL manuals. Non-reserved words, such as table and column names, are written in lower case.

In the book examples a single space is used between words or expressions. Extra spaces are allowed and have no effect.

Code Download

The examples accompanying this book can be downloaded from the publisher's website:

http://books.brainysoftware.com/download

Chapter 1
Storing and Maintaining Data

Data in a relational database (such as the Oracle database) is stored in tables. A very simple **sales** database, for example, might have four tables that store data on products, customers, suppliers, and customer orders.

When you add a record of data into a table, the record is stored as a row of the table. A record has fields. A **product** record, for example, might have four fields: product code, name, price, and launch date. All records you store in the **product** table must have the same fields. Each of the fields is a column of the table.

This chapter shows you how to use SQL statements to store and maintain data. The main objective of this chapter is to give you a taste of working with SQL.

To test the book examples you need a working Oracle database. Appendix A, "Installing Oracle Database XE" shows how you can install Oracle Database Express Edition (XE) and make it ready for use with the examples. This appendix also shows you how to use SQL*Plus to execute your SQL statements. If you do not have a working Oracle database, you should read Appendix A first.

Selecting A Database to Use

You need a database to store your data. When you install Oracle Database XE, a database named "XE" is created as part of the installation. To use this database, run SQL*Plus and issue a CONNECT command as described in Appendix A, "Installing Oracle Database XE."

Creating a Table

Before you can store data in a database, you must first create a table for your data. You do this by using the SQL CREATE TABLE statement. Tables that you create will reside in the database that you are currently connected to, which in this case is the XE database.

The syntax for the CREATE TABLE statement is as follows.

```
CREATE TABLE table
    (column_1 data_type_1,
    column_2 data_type_2,
    ...
    PRIMARY KEY (columns)
);
```

Listing 1.1 shows a CREATE TABLE statement for creating a **product** table with four columns.

Listing 1.1: Creating a product table with four columns
```
CREATE TABLE product
  (
    p_code    VARCHAR2(6),
    p_name    VARCHAR2(15),
    price     NUMBER(4,2),
    launch_dt DATE,
    PRIMARY KEY (p_code)
  );
```

The four columns have three different data types. They are as follows.

- VARCHAR2(n): variable length string up to n characters.
- NUMBER(p, s): numeric with precision p and scale s. The **price** column, whose type is NUMBER(4,2), can store numbers between -99.99 and +99.99.
- DATE, a date.

Note
Appendix B, "Oracle Built-in Data Types" provides a complete list of Oracle data types.

When creating a table, you should always add a primary key, even though a primary key is optional. A primary key is a column or a set of columns that uniquely identify every row in the table. In the CREATE TABLE statement in Listing 1.1, the **p_code** field will be made the primary key for the **product** table.

Also note that an SQL statement must be terminated with a semicolon (;)

Copying the Table Structure

Another way of creating a table is by copying the structure of an existing table using the CREATE TABLE statement with the following syntax.

```
CREATE TABLE table AS
SELECT * FROM source_table;
```

Listing 1.2 is an SQL statement that creates an **old_product** table from the **product** table.

Listing 1.2: Copying table
```
CREATE TABLE old_product AS
SELECT * FROM product;
```

The statement in Listing 1.2 creates the **old_product** table by copying the structure (columns) of the **product** table along with its rows. If you want to copy the structure only, add a WHERE clause like the statement in Listing 1.3.

Listing 1.3: Creating the table structure only
```
CREATE TABLE old_product AS
SELECT * FROM product WHERE P_CODE = NULL;
```

Constraints

A constraint is a rule to which data must conform. A primary key, for instance, is a constraint. A primary key column must have a value (cannot be NULL) and the value must be unique throughout the table. A primary key can be a combination of columns, in which case none of the column can be null and their combination must be unique.

In addition to primary key, you can also apply NOT NULL, UNIQUE and CHECK constraint. In Listing 1.4 we apply a primary key constraint to the **p_code** column, UNIQUE to **p_name**, CHECK to **price**, and NOT NULL to **launch_dt**.

Listing 1.4: Using Constraints

```
CREATE TABLE new_product
  (
    p_code VARCHAR2(6) PRIMARY KEY,
    p_name VARCHAR2(15) UNIQUE,
    price  NUMBER(4,2) CHECK (price < 100.00),
    launch_dt DATE NOT NULL
  );
```

If after creating the **new_product** table you try to insert a row that violates any of the rule, the row will be rejected. For example, if you try to insert a row that has a price equal or larger than 100.00 you will get the following error message.

```
SQL Error: ORA-01438: value larger than specified precision allowed for
this column
```

Synonyms

A table name may be up to 30 characters long, and long table names may be too impractical or cryptic. You can provide a friendly name for a table by creating a synonym.

The syntax of the statement for creating a synonym is as follows.

```
CREATE PUBLIC SYNONYM synonym
FOR table;
```

The PUBLIC keyword is used to make the synonym accessible to all users. The statement in Listing 1.5 creates a synonym **new_prod** for the **new_product** table.

Listing 1.5: Creating new_prod synonym

```
CREATE PUBLIC SYNONYM new_prod FOR new_product;
```

Note that to use a synonym, the user must have the required permission on the table.

Another scenario whereby a synonym is typically used is when a table owner wants other users to be able to use his or her table without having to prefix the table with the owner's user name. The statement in Listing 1.6 creates a synonym for the **product** table created by user **djoni**, so other users can just refer the table as **product** without the **djoni.** prefix.

Listing 1.6: Creating a synonym for the product table

```
CREATE PUBLIC SYNONYM product FOR djoni.product;
```

Adding Data

Once you have a table, you can add data to it using the INSERT statement. The syntax for the INSERT statement is as follows.

```
INSERT INTO table
   (column_1,
    column_2,
    ... )
VALUES (value_1,
        value_2,
     ... )
);
```

For example, Listing 1.7 shows an SQL statement that inserts a row into the **product** table.

Listing 1.7: Inserting a row into the product table

```
INSERT INTO product
   ( p_code, p_name, price, launch_dt)
   VALUES ( 1, 'Nail', 10.0, '31-MAR-2013');
```

If you get an error message due to the wrong date format, execute the following statement, and then re-execute the INSERT statement.

```
ALTER SESSION
SET NLS_DATE_FORMAT = 'DD-MON_YYYY';
```

After you execute the statement in Listing 1.6, your **product** table will have one row. You can query your table using this statement.

```
SELECT * FROM product;
```

The query result will be as follows.

```
P_CODE P_NAME     PRICE LAUNCH_DT
------ ---------- ------ ---------
1      Nail       10.00 31-MAR-13
```

You can only add one row with the INSERT statement. The five INSERT statements in Listing 1.8 add five more rows to the **product** table.

Listing 1.8: Adding five more rows to the product table

```
INSERT INTO product ( p_code, p_name, price, launch_dt)
   VALUES (2, 'Washer', 15.00, '29-MAR-2013');
INSERT INTO product ( p_code, p_name, price, launch_dt)
   VALUES (3, 'Nut', 15.00, '29-MAR-13');
INSERT INTO product ( p_code, p_name, price, launch_dt)
   VALUES (4, 'Screw', 25.00, '30-MAR-2013');
INSERT INTO product (p_code, p_name, price, launch_dt)
   VALUES (5, 'Super_Nut', 30.00, '30-MAR-2013');
INSERT INTO product (p_code, p_name, price, launch_dt)
   VALUES (6, 'New Nut', NULL, NULL);
```

After executing the statements in Listing 1.8, your **product** table will contain these rows.

```
P_CODE P_NAME       PRICE LAUNCH_DT
------ ----------   ------ ---------
1      Nail         10.00 31-MAR-13
2      Washer       15.00 29-MAR-13
3      Nut          15.00 29-MAR-13
4      Screw        25.00 30-MAR-13
5      Super_Nut    30.00 30-MAR-13
6      New Nut      NULL   NULL
```

Now issue a COMMIT command to persist (confirm the storage of) the additional five rows.

```
COMMIT;
```

> **Note**
> You need to run the COMMIT statement after INSERT, UPDATE, and DELETE to persist the data changes.

Copying Data

Another way to add data is by copying data from another table using the INSERT statement with the following syntax.

```
INSERT INTO table
    (column_1,
     column_2,
     ... )
SELECT value_1,
       value_2,
    ...
FROM source_table)
);
```

Assuming you have an **old_product** table, you can execute the the INSERT statement in Listing 1.9 to copy all rows from the **old_product** table into the **product** table.

Listing 1.9: Copying data from the old_product table
```
INSERT INTO product
  (P_CODE, P_NAME, PRICE, LAUNCH_DT
  )
SELECT P_CODE, P_NAME, PRICE, LAUNCH_DT FROM old_product;
```

To try the above statement, insert four rows using the statements in Listing 1.10.

Listing 1.10: Adding data into old_product table
```
INSERT INTO old_product ( p_code, p_name, price, launch_dt)
  VALUES (20, 'Ring', 10.00, '29-MAR-2009');
INSERT INTO old_product ( p_code, p_name, price, launch_dt)
  VALUES (30, 'Tire', 20.00, '29-MAR-2010');
INSERT INTO old_product ( p_code, p_name, price, launch_dt)
  VALUES (30, 'Hammer', 20.50, '29-MAR-2011');
INSERT INTO old_product (p_code, p_name, price, launch_dt)
```

```
VALUES (40, 'Paint', 30.75, '30-MAR-2010');
```

After executing the statements in Listing 1.10, your **product** table will contain the following rows.

```
P_CODE P_NAME        PRICE LAUNCH_DT
------ ---------- ------ ---------
1      Nail          10.00 31-MAR-13
2      Washer        15.00 29-MAR-13
3      Nut           15.00 29-MAR-13
4      Screw         25.00 30-MAR-13
5      Super_Nut     30.00 30-MAR-13
6      New Nut       NULL  NULL
20     Ring          10.00 29-MAR-09
30     Tire          20.00 29-MAR-10
40     Hammer        20.50 29-MAR-11
50     Paint         30.75 30-MAR-10
```

We do not want to persist the four additional rows in the **product** table, so we issue a ROLLBACK command.

```
ROLLBACK;
```

If you want to copy only selected rows, add a WHERE clause. Its condition determines the rows that will be selected and copied over.

For example, the statement in Listing 1.11 copies only old products that were launched before 2011.

Listing 1.11: Copying selective rows

```
INSERT INTO product
  (P_CODE, P_NAME, PRICE, LAUNCH_DT
  )
SELECT P_CODE, P_NAME, PRICE, LAUNCH_DT FROM old_product
WHERE (launched_dt, 'YYYY') < 2011;
```

Multitable Insert

Using the INSERT statement you can add data into more than one table. The multitable insert syntax is as follows.

```
INSERT ALL
WHEN condition1 THEN
INTO table1 (column11, column12, ...)
VALUES (value11, value12, ...)
WHEN condition2 THEN
INTO table2 (column21, column22, ...)
VALUES (value21, value22, ...)
...
ELSE
INTO tableN (columnN1, columnN2, ...)
SELECT ... FROM table ...
;
```

The statement in Listing 1.12 adds data from the **product** table into **old_product** and **new_product** tables.

Listing 1.12: Copying selective rows
```
INSERT ALL
  WHEN launch_dt <= to_date
  ('30-03-13','DD-MM-YY')
  THEN INTO old_product VALUES
  (P_CODE, P_NAME, PRICE, LAUNCH_DT
  )
  ELSE INTO new_product VALUES
  (P_CODE, P_NAME, PRICE, LAUNCH_DT
  )
SELECT P_CODE, P_NAME, PRICE, LAUNCH_DT FROM product;
```

Updating Data

You use the UPDATE statement to update one or more columns of existing data. You can update all rows in a table or certain rows only.

The syntax for the UPDATE statement is as follows

```
UPDATE table_name
SET column_1 = new_value_1 [,
    column_2 = new_value_2,
    ... ]
[WHERE condition];
```

You specify which rows to update in a WHERE clause. Without a WHERE clause, all rows will be updated. With a WHERE clause, only rows that meet the condition will be updated. If no row meets the condition in the WHERE clause, nothing will be updated.

As an example, the SQL statement in Listing 1.13 will cut the price by 5%. As the UPDATE statement does not have a WHERE clause, the prices of all the products will be updated.

Listing 1.13: Updating the price column
```
UPDATE product
SET price = price - (price * 0.05);
```

If you query the product table using this statement, you will learn that the values in the **price** column have changed.

```
SELECT * FROM product;
```

Here is the result of the query.

```
P_CODE P_NAME      PRICE LAUNCH_DT
------ ---------- ------ ---------
1      Nail        9.50 31-MAR-13
2      Washer     14.25 29-MAR-13
3      Nut        14.25 29-MAR-13
4      Screw      23.75 30-MAR-13
```

```
5        Super_Nut   28.50 30-MAR-13
6        New Nut     NULL    NULL
```

Now, issue a ROLLBACK command to return the **price** values back to before the update:

```
ROLLBACK;
```

As another example, the statement in Listing 1.14 updates the price of product with p_code = 9. Since the **product** table does not have such a p_code, no row will be updated.

Listing 1.14: Updating the price column with a WHERE clause

```
UPDATE product
SET price = price - (price * 0.05)
WHERE p_code = 9;
```

Deleting Data

To delete a row or multiple rows in a table, use the DELETE statement. You can specify which rows to delete by using the WHERE clause.

The syntax for the DELETE statement is as follows

```
DELETE FROM table
[WHERE condition];
```

You specify which rows to delete in the WHERE clause.

For example, the statement in Listing 1.15 deletes from the **product** table all rows whose **p_name** field value is 'Nut'.

Listing 1.15: Deleting rows

```
DELETE FROM product
WHERE p_name = 'Nut';
```

After you run the statement in Listing 1.15, please issue a ROLLBACK command to return the data values back to before the deletion:

```
ROLLBACK;
```

If none of the rows meets the condition, nothing will be deleted.

Note that you cannot delete some of the columns in a row; the DELETE statement deletes the whole row. If you need to change the content of a specific column, use the UPDATE statement. For instance, the statement in Listing 1.16 changes the content of the **price** column to NULL. NULL is the absence of a value; it is neither 0 (zero) or empty. Chapter 2, "Basic Queries" explains NULL in detail.

Listing 1.16: Updating to NULL

```
UPDATE product SET price = NULL WHERE p_name = 'Nut';
```

When you query the Nut product, the result will show NULL on the price column.

```
SELECT * FROM product WHERE p_name = 'Nut';
```

The output is as follows.

```
P_CODE P_NAME  PRICE LAUNCH_DT
------ ------  ------ ---------
1      Nut     NULL   13-DEC-01
```

Please issue a ROLLBACK command to return the data values back to before the update:

```
ROLLBACK;
```

NULL display
In SQL* Plus, the default display of NULL is blank. Throughout this book, NULL is displayed as NULL. You can change the setting by executing the **SET null NULL** command in your SQL*Plus console.

Truncating Data

While you can delete all rows using the DELETE statement that does not have a WHERE condition, a TRUNCATE statement is faster and it does not require a COMMIT statement. Listing 1.17 is an example TRUNCATE statement.

Listing 1.17: Truncating old_product table
```
TRUNCATE TABLE old_product;
```

Note that you cannot rollback (recover) truncated data.

The MERGE statement

Using the MERGE statement you can add, update, and delete data, in a table. Its syntax is as follows.

```
MERGE INTO table
USING source_data
ON ( condition )
WHEN MATCHED THEN UPDATE SET column1=value1, column2=value2, ...
[DELETE WHERE where_clause]
WHEN NOT MATCHED THEN INSERT (column1, column2, ...) VALUES (value1,
     value2, ...);
```

The MATCHED or NOT MATCHED test is the result of evaluating the ON condition. The DELETE clause is optional. If the DELETE clause is present, those rows that MATCHED **and** meet *where_clause* will be deleted. *source_data* can be a table or a query.

Listing 1.18 presents an example MERGE statement that updates, deletes, and adds data. The source_data is the **old_product** table.

Listing 1.18: MERGE into product table
```
MERGE INTO product p USING old_product op ON (p.p_code=op.p_code AND
     TO_CHAR(p.launch_dt, 'YYYYMMDD') < '20130331')
WHEN MATCHED THEN
  UPDATE SET p.price=op.price
```

```
      DELETE WHERE p.price < 15.00
 WHEN NOT MATCHED THEN
   INSERT
     (p_code, p_name
     ) VALUES
     ('OLD'||op.p_code, 'TBD'
     ) ;
```

Assume the **product** table contains the following rows

```
P_CODE P_NAME      PRICE LAUNCH_DT
------ ----------  ----- ---------
1      Nail        10.00 31-MAR-13
2      Washer      15.00 29-MAR-13
3      Nut         15.00 29-MAR-13
4      Screw       25.00 30-MAR-13
5      Super_Nut   30.00 30-MAR-13
6      New Nut     NULL  NULL
```

and the **old_product** table has the following rows

```
P_CODE P_NAME      PRICE LAUNCH_DT
------ ----------  ----- ---------
1      Nail         5.00 31-MAR-13
2      Washer      10.00 29-MAR-13
4      Screw       20.00 29-MAR-13
```

Since only Washer and Screw meet the merge condition, their prices are updated to 10.00 and 25.00, respectively. However, Washer meets the where condition of the DELETE clause, so it will be deleted.

After executing Listing 1.18, the **product** table will have the following rows.

```
P_CODE P_NAME      PRICE LAUNCH_DT
------ ----------  ----- ---------
1      Nail        10.00 31-MAR-13
3      Nut         15.00 29-MAR-13
4      Screw       20.00 30-MAR-13
5      Super_Nut   30.00 30-MAR-13
6      New Nut     NULL  NULL
OLD1   TBD         NULL  NULL
```

We do not want to persist the changes, so please issue a ROLLBACK statement.

Altering A Table

You can rename a table, rename or change its column using the ALTER TABLE statement. The statements in Listing 1.19 rename the **old_product** table, rename the **p_name** column of the **older_product** table, change the size of the **price** column, remove the **launch_dt** column, and add the **launch_dt** column back.

Listing 1.19: Alter Table statements
```
ALTER ALTER TABLE old_product RENAME TO older_product;
ALTER TABLE older_product RENAME COLUMN p_name TO prod_nam;
ALTER TABLE older_product MODIFY price NUMBER(6,2);
ALTER TABLE older_product DROP COLUMN launch_dt;
ALTER TABLE older_product ADD launch_dt DATE;
```

Deleting A Table

When you no longer need a table in the database, you can delete it using the DROP TABLE statement. For example, the statement in Listing 1.20 deletes the **old_product** table from the database.

Listing 1.20: Dropping old_product table
```
DROP TABLE old_product;
```

Summary

In this chapter you got the first taste of working with SQL. You learned how to create a table and store data. In Chapter 2, "Basic Queries" you will learn to use the SELECT statement to query data.

Chapter 2
Basic Queries

A query is a request for data from one or more tables. When you execute a query, rows that satisfy the query condition are returned as a table. Similarly, when a query embedded in another query or a program gets executed, the data retrieved is returned as a table to the other query or program.

In this chapter you learn how to write basic queries using the SELECT statement. Once you master the basic queries, you can start learning about queries within other queries in Chapter 6, "Subqueries" and within PL/SQL programs in Chapter 10, "PL/SQL."

The SELECT statement

All queries regardless of their complexity use the SELECT statement. The SELECT statement has the following general syntax.

```
SELECT column_names FROM table_name [WHERE condition];
```

Only the SELECT and FROM clauses are mandatory. If your query does not have a WHERE clause, the result will include all rows in the table. If your query has a WHERE clause then only the rows meeting the WHERE condition will be returned.

Querying All Data

The simplest query, which reads all data (all rows and all columns) from a table, has the following syntax.

```
SELECT * FROM table;
```

The asterisk (*) means all columns in the table. For instance, Listing 2.1 shows an SQL statement that queries all data from the **product** table.

Listing 2.1: Querying all product data
```
SELECT * FROM product;
```

Executing the query will give you the following result.

```
P_CODE P_NAME       PRICE LAUNCH_DT
------ ----------   ------ ---------
1      Nail         10.00 31-MAR-13
2      Washer       15.00 29-MAR-13
3      Nut          15.00 29-MAR-13
4      Screw        25.00 30-MAR-13
5      Super_Nut    30.00 30-MAR-13
6      New Nut      NULL  NULL
```

Selecting Specific Columns

To query specific columns, list the columns in the SELECT clause. You write the columns in the order you want to see them in the output table. For example, the SELECT statement in Listing 2.2 queries the **p_name** and the **price** columns from the **product** table.

Listing 2.2: Querying specific columns
```
SELECT p_name, price FROM product;
```

The query will return the **p_name** and **price** columns in all rows. Here is the query output.

```
P_NAME       PRICE
----------   ------
Nail         10.00
Washer       15.00
Nut          15.00
Screw        25.00
Super_Nut    30.00
New Nut      NULL
```

Selecting Rows with WHERE

To query specific rows, use the WHERE clause. Recall that the SQL SELECT statement has the following syntax.

```
SELECT column_names FROM table_name [WHERE condition];
```

For example, the SQL statement in Listing 2.3 queries the **p_name** and **price** data from the **product** table with price = 15.

Listing 2.3: Querying specific rows
```
SELECT p_name, price FROM product WHERE price = 15;
```

Only rows whose price is 15 will be returned by the query, in this case the Washer and Nut. The query output is as follows.

```
P_NAME      PRICE
---------   ------
Washer      15.00
Nut         15.00
```

The equal sign (=) in the WHERE condition in Listing 2.3 is one of the comparison operators. Table 2.1 shows all comparison operators.

Operator	Description
=	Equal to
<	Less than
>	Greater than
<=	Less than or equal to
>=	Greater than or equal to
!=	Not equal to

Table 2.1: Comparison operators

As another example, Listing 2.4 shows a WHERE clause that uses the not equal to (!=) operator.

Listing 2.4: Using the != comparison operator

```
SELECT p_name, price FROM product WHERE p_name != 'Nut';
```

Only rows whose **p_name** value is not Nut will be returned by the query. In this case, the query output will be as follows.

```
P_NAME      PRICE
---------   ------
Nail        10.00
Washer      15.00
Screw       25.00
Super_Nut   30.00
New Nut     NULL
```

Compound Conditions

The condition p_name != 'Nut' in Listing 2.4 is called a predicate. Using the AND and OR logical operator you can combine predicates to form a compound condition. Only rows that satisfy the compound condition will be returned by the query.

The rules for the OR logical operator are given in Table 2.2.

Left condition	Logical operator	Right condition	Compound condition
True	OR	True	True
True	OR	False	True
False	OR	True	True
False	OR	False	False

Table 2.2: The rules for OR

In principle, the result of the OR compound condition is true (satisfying the condition) if any one of the two conditions being OR-ed is true; otherwise, if none of the conditions is true, the compound condition is false (not satisfying the condition).

The rules for the AND logical operator are presented in Table 2.3.

Left condition	Logical operator	Right condition	Compound condition
True	AND	True	True
True	AND	False	FALSE
False	AND	True	FALSE
False	AND	False	FALSE

Table 2.3: The AND rules

Basically, the result of the AND compound condition is true only if the two conditions being AND-ed are true; otherwise, the result is false.

For example, the statement in Listing 2.5 contains three predicates in its WHERE clause.

Listing 2.5: A query with three predicates

```
SELECT *
FROM product
WHERE (launch_dt >= '30-MAR-13'
OR price       > 15)
AND (p_name    != 'Nail');
```

The result of the first compound condition (launch_dt >= '30-MAR-13' OR price > 15) is true for Nail, Screw and Super_Nut rows in the **product** table; AND-ing this result with the (p_name != 'Nail') predicate results in two products, the Screw and Super_Nut.

Here is the output of the query in Listing 2.5:

```
P_CODE P_NAME       PRICE LAUNCH_DT
------ ----------- ------ ---------

4      Screw        25.00 30-MAR-13
5      Super_Nut    30.00 30-MAR-13
```

Note that New Nut does not satisfy the condition because applying any of the comparison operators to NULL results in false (the **price** and **launch_dt** values of the New Nut are NULL). The section "Handling NULL" later in this chapter explains more about NULL.

Operator Precedence

If a compound condition contains both the OR and the AND conditions, the AND condition will be evaluated first because AND has a higher precedence than OR. However, anything in parentheses will have an even higher precedence than AND. For example, the SELECT statement in Listing 2.5 has an OR and an AND, but the OR condition is in parentheses so the OR condition will be evaluated first. If you remove the parentheses in the SELECT statement in Listing 2.5, the query will return a different result. Consider the statement in Listing 2.6, which is similar to that in Listing 2.5 except that the parentheses have been removed.

Listing 2.6: Evaluation precedence

```
SELECT *
FROM product
WHERE launch_dt >= '30-MAR-13'
OR price         > 15
AND p_name       != 'Nail';
```

For your reading convenience, the content of the **product** table is reprinted here.

```
P_CODE P_NAME       PRICE LAUNCH_DT
------ ---------- ------ ---------
1      Nail        10.00 31-MAR-13
2      Washer      15.00 29-MAR-13
3      Nut         15.00 29-MAR-13
4      Screw       25.00 30-MAR-13
5      Super_Nut   30.00 30-MAR-13
6      New Nut     NULL  NULL
```

Without parentheses, the compound condition price > 15 AND p_name != 'Nail' will be evaluated first, resulting in the Screw and Super_Nut. The result is then OR-ed with the launch_dt >= 30-MAR-13' condition, resulting in these three rows.

```
P_CODE P_NAME       PRICE LAUNCH_DT
------ ---------- ------ ---------
1      Nail        10.00 31-MAR-13
4      Screw       25.00 30-MAR-13
5      Super_Nut   30.00 30-MAR-13
```

The NOT logical operator

You can use NOT to negate a condition and return rows that do not satisfy the condition. Consider the query in Listing 2.7.

Listing 2.7: Using the NOT operator

```
SELECT *
FROM product
WHERE NOT (launch_dt >= '30-MAR-13'
OR price         > 15
AND p_name       != 'Nail' );
```

Thanks to the NOT operator in the query in Listing 2.7, the two rows not satisfying the condition in Listing 2.6 will now be returned.

```
P_CODE P_NAME       PRICE LAUNCH_DT
------ --------- ------ ---------
2      Washer     15.00 29-MAR-13
3      Nut        15.00 29-MAR-13
```

As another example, the query in Listing 2.8 negates the last predicate only (as opposed to the previous query that negated the overall WHERE condition).

Listing 2.8: Using NOT on one predicate
```
SELECT *
FROM product
WHERE (launch_dt >= '30-MAR-13'
OR price        > 15)
AND NOT (p_name  != 'Nail');
```

The output of the query in Listing 2.8 is as follows.

```
P_CODE P_NAME      PRICE LAUNCH_DT
------ ---------   ------ ---------
1      Nail        10.00 31-MAR-13
```

The BETWEEN Operator

The BETWEEN operator evaluates equality to any value within a range. The range is specified by a boundary, which specifies the lowest and the highest values.

Here is the syntax for BETWEEN.

```
SELECT columns FROM table
WHERE column BETWEEN(lowest_value, highest_value);
```

The boundary values are inclusive, meaning *lowest_value* and *highest_value* will be included in the equality evaluation.

For example, the query in Listing 2.9 uses the BETWEEN operator to specify the lowest and highest prices that need to be returned from the product table.

Listing 2.9: Using the BETWEEN operator
```
SELECT * FROM product WHERE price BETWEEN 15 AND 25;
```

Here is the output of the query in Listing 2.9.

```
P_CODE P_NAME      PRICE LAUNCH_DT
------ ---------   ------ ---------
2      Washer      15.00 29-MAR-13
3      Nut         15.00 29-MAR-13
4      Screw       25.00 30-MAR-13
```

The IN Operator

The IN operator compares a column with a list of values. The syntax for a query that uses IN is as follows.

```
SELECT columns FROM table
WHERE column IN(value1, value2, ...);
```

For example, the query in Listing 2.10 uses the IN operator to select all columns whose price is in the list (10, 25, 50).

Listing 2.10: Using the IN operator

```
SELECT * FROM product WHERE price IN (10, 25, 50);
```

The output of the query in Listing 2.10 is as follows.

```
P_CODE P_NAME      PRICE LAUNCH_DT
------ ---------   ------ ---------
1      Nail        10.00 31-MAR-13
4      Screw       25.00 30-MAR-13
```

The LIKE Operator

The LIKE operator allows you to specify an imprecise equality condition. The syntax is as follows.

```
SELECT columns FROM table
WHERE column LIKE ' ... wildcard_character ... ';
```

The wildcard character can be a percentage sign (%) to represent any number of characters or an underscore (_) to represent a single occurrence of any character.

As an example, the query in Listing 2.11 uses the LIKE operator to find products whose name starts with N and is followed by two other characters plus products whose name starts with Sc and can be of any length.

Listing 2.11: Using the LIKE operator

```
SELECT * FROM product WHERE p_name LIKE 'N__' OR p_name LIKE 'Sc%';
```

The output of the query in Listing 2.11 is this.

```
P_CODE P_NAME      PRICE LAUNCH_DT
------ ---------   ------ ---------
3      Nut         15.00 29-MAR-13
4      Screw       25.00 30-MAR-13
```

Even though you can use LIKE for numeric columns, it is primarily used with columns of type string.

Escaping the Wildcard Character

If the string you specify in the LIKE operator contains an underscore or a percentage sign, SQL will regard it as a wild character. For example, if you want to query products that have an underscore in their names, your SQL statement would look like that in Listing 2.12.

Listing 2.12: A wildcard character _ in the LIKE string

```
SELECT * FROM product WHERE p_name LIKE '%_%';
```

If you execute the query in Listing 2.12, the query will return all rows instead of just Super_Nut, because the underscore in the LIKE operator is regarded as a wild card character, i.e. any one character. Listing 2.13 resolves this problem by prefixing the wild card character with an ESCAPE character. In the statement the ESCAPE clause defines \ (backslash) as an escape character, meaning any character in the LIKE operator after a backslash will be considered a character, not as a wildcard character. Now only rows whose p_name contains an underscore will be returned.

Listing 2.13: Escaping the wildcard character _

```
SELECT * FROM product WHERE p_name LIKE '%\_%' ESCAPE '\';
```

The query in Listing 2.13 will produce the following output.

```
P_CODE P_NAME    PRICE LAUNCH_DT
------ --------- ------ ---------
5      Super_Nut 30.00 30-MAR-13
```

Combining the NOT operator

You can combine NOT with BETWEEN, IN, or LIKE to negate their conditions. For example, the query in Listing 2.14 uses NOT with BETWEEN.

Listing 2.14: Using NOT with BETWEEN

```
SELECT * FROM product WHERE price NOT BETWEEN 15 AND 25;
```

Executing the query in Listing 2.14 will give you this result.

```
P_CODE P_NAME    PRICE LAUNCH_DT
------ --------- ------ ---------
1      Nail      10.00 31-MAR-13
5      Super_Nut 30.00 30-MAR-13
```

Handling NULLNULL, an SQL reserved word, represents the absence of data. NULL is applicable to any data type. It is not the same as a numeric zero or an empty string or a 0000/00/00 date. You can specify whether or not a column can be null in the CREATE TABLE statement for creating the table.

The result of applying any of the comparison operators on NULL is always NULL. You can only test whether or not a column is NULL by using the IS NULL or IS NOT NULL operator.

Consider the query in Listing 2.15.

Listing 2.15: Invalid usage of the equal operator on NULL

```
SELECT * FROM product WHERE price = NULL;
```

Executing the query in Listing 2.15 produces no output. In fact, you will get the following message.

```
no rows selected
```

As another example, consider the query in Listing 2.16 that uses IS NULL.

Listing 2.16: Using IS NULL

```
SELECT * FROM product WHERE price IS NULL;
```

The query output is as follows.

```
P_NO P_NAME      PRICE LAUNCH_DT
---- ---------  ------ ---------
6    New Nut    NULL   NULL
```

Note
Chapter 6, "Built-in Functions," discusses functions that you can use to test column nullity.

Summary

In this chapter you learned about basics queries using the SELECT statement. In the next chapter you will learn how to format query outputs.

Chapter 3
Query Output

All the queries in Chapter 2, "Basic Queries" returned rows that contained columns from the source table. However, output rows can also contain string or numeric expressions that include string or numeric literals, operators, and functions.

In this chapter you learn how to manipulate query output using expressions and how to order and store output rows into a table.

Column Aliases

By default the names of the output columns in a query output are the names of the columns of the queried table. However, you don't have to be stuck with the original column names. You can give them different names or aliases if you wish.

The syntax for the SELECT clause that uses aliases is as follows.

```
SELECT column_1 AS alias1, column_2 AS alias2, ...
FROM table;
```

An alias can consist of one or multiple words. You must enclose a multiword alias with quotes, e.g. "PRODUCT NAME". For example, the query in Listing 3.1 uses an alias for the **p_name** column.

Listing 3.1: Using an alias in a query
```
SELECT p_code,
  p_name AS "PRODUCT NAME"
FROM product;
```

Expressions

An output column can also be an expression. An expression in the SELECT clause can include columns, literal values, arithmetic or string operators, and functions. For instance, the SELECT clause in the query in Listing 3.2 employs several expressions.

Listing 3.2: Various types of output columns
```
SELECT p_code,
  'p_name in Uppercase: '
```

```
   || UPPER(p_name)                    AS "PRODUCT NAME",
   (price * 100)                       AS "NORMALIZED_PRICE",
   TO_CHAR(launch_dt, 'DD/MM/YYYY') AS "LAUNCH_DATE"
FROM product;
```

The output of the query in Listing 3.2 will have four columns.

The first output column, **p_code**, is a column from the product table.

The second output column (aliased "PRODUCT NAME") is an expression that contains three parts, a literal 'p_name in Uppercase: ', a concatenation string operator (||), and UPPER(p_name). The latter, UPPER, is a function applied to the p_name column from the product table. The UPPER function changes the case of the product names to uppercase.

The third output column ("NORMALIZED_PRICE") is an arithmetic expression (price*100).

The last output column ("LAUNCH_DATE") is the launch_date column formatted as DD/MM/YYYY.

Applied against the following **product** table

```
P_CODE P_NAME            PRICE LAUNCH_DT
------ ---------------- ----- ---- ----
1      Nail             10.00 31-MAR-13
2      Washer           15.00 29-MAR-13
3      Nut              15.00 29-MAR-13
4      Screw            25.00 30-MAR-13
5      Super_Nut        30.00 30-MAR-13
6      New Nut                NULL NULL
```

the query in Listing 3.2 returns the following rows.

```
P_CODE PRODUCT NAME                    NORMALIZED_PRICE LAUNCH_DATE
------ ------------------------------- ---------------- -----------
1      p_name in Uppercase: NAIL                   1000 31/03/2013
2      p_name in Uppercase: WASHER                 1500 29/03/2013
3      p_name in Uppercase: NUT                    1500 29/03/2013
4      p_name in Uppercase: SCREW                  2500 30/03/2013
5      p_name in Uppercase: SUPER_NUT              3000 30/03/2013
6      p_name in Uppercase: NEW NUT            NULL NULL
```

You can use other arithmetic operators in addition to the multiplication (*) operator in your column. These include addition (+), subtraction (-), and division (/)

Note
Chapter 9, "Built-in Functions" explains functions in more detail.

Limiting the Number of Rows

You can limit the number of output rows by using the ROWNUM pseudo column. Its syntax is as follows.

```
SELECT columns FROM table(s)
WHERE conditions AND ROWNUM < count;
```

The maximum number of output rows of a query that employs ROWNUM will be *count* – 1.

As an example, take a look at the query in Listing 3.3.

Listing 3.3: Using ROWNUM

SELECT * FROM product WHERE price > 10 AND ROWNUM < 4;

Without the expression ROWNUM < 4, the number of output rows would be 4. The query in Listing 3.3, however, returns these three rows.

```
P_CODE P_NAME           PRICE LAUNCH_DT
------ ---------------- ----- ---- ---------
2      Washer           15.00 29-MAR-13
3      Nut              15.00 29-MAR-13
4      Screw            25.00 30-MAR-13
```

The DISTINCT Keyword

A query may return duplicate rows. Two rows are duplicates if each of their columns contains exactly the same data. If you don't want to see duplicate output rows, use DISTINCT in your SELECT clause. You can use DISTINCT on one column or multiple columns.

Using DISTINCT on A Single Column

The query in Listing 3.4 uses DISTINCT on the price column.

Listing 3.4: Using DISTINCT on a single column
```
SELECT DISTINCT price FROM product ORDER BY price;
```

Without DISTINCT, the query in Listing 3.4 will return six rows that include two duplicate prices for row 2 and row 3. Instead, the query in Listing 3.4 returns the following output.

```
PRICE
-----
   10
   15
   25
   30
NULL
```

Using DISTINCT on Multiple Columns

If a query returns multiple columns, two rows are considered duplicates if all their columns have the same values. They are not duplicates if only one column has the same value.

The DISTINCT keyword can be applied on multiple columns too. For example, the query in Listing 3.5 uses DISTINCT on multiple columns.

Listing 3.5: Using DISTINCT on multiple columns

```
SELECT DISTINCT price, launch_dt FROM product ORDER BY price;
```

Here is the output. Note that output rows with the same price and launch_dt will only be shown once.

```
PRICE LAUNCH_DT
----- ---------
   10 31-MAR-13
   15 29-MAR-13
   25 30-MAR-13
   30 30-MAR-13
NULL  NULL
```

Aggregate Functions

You can manipulate your query output further by using aggregate functions. The aggregate functions are listed in Table 3.1.

Function	Description
MAX(column)	The maximum column value
MIN(column)	The minimum column value
SUM(column)	The sum of column values
AVG(column)	The average column value
COUNT(column)	The count of rows
COUNT(*)	The count of all rows including NULL.

Table 3.1: Built-in aggregate functions

As an example, the query in Listing 3.6 uses the aggregate functions in Table 3.1.

Listing 3.6: Using aggregate functions

```
SELECT MAX(price),
  MIN(price),
  SUM(price),
  AVG(price),
  COUNT(price),
  COUNT(*)
FROM product;
```

Note that only COUNT(*) takes into account the New Nut product because its price is NULL.

The output of the query in Listing 3.6 is this.

```
MAX(PRICE) MIN(PRICE) SUM(PRICE) AVG(PRICE) COUNT(PRICE)   COUNT(*)
---------- ---------- ---------- ---------- ------------ ----------
        30         10         95         19            5          6
```

The CASE expressionCASE allows you to have dynamic query output in which a column value may vary depending on the value of the column. CASE comes in two flavors: Simple and Searched. Both will be explained in the following subsections.

The Simple CASE

The general syntax for the Simple CASE is as follows.

```
SELECT columns,
  CASE column
    WHEN equal_value1
    THEN output_value1
    WHEN equal_value2
    THEN output_value2
    WHEN ...
    [ELSE else_value]
  END AS output_column
FROM table
WHERE ... ;
```

In the Simple CASE, *column_name* is compared to *equal_value*s in the WHEN clause, starting from the first WHEN and down to the last WHEN. If *column_name* matches a WHEN value, the value right after the THEN clause is returned and the CASE process stops. If *column_name* matches none of the WHEN values, *else_value* is returned if there exists an ELSE clause. If *column_name* matches none of the WHEN values but no ELSE clause exists, NULL will be returned.

As an example, the query in Listing 3.7 uses a Simple CASE expression for the price column to produce a price_cat (price category) output column.

Listing 3.7: An example of the Simple CASE
```
SELECT p_code,
  p_name,
  CASE price
    WHEN 10
    THEN 'Cheap'
    WHEN 15
    THEN 'Medium'
    WHEN 25
    THEN 'Expensive'
    ELSE 'Others'
  END AS price_cat
FROM product;
```

Assuming the **product** table has the following data

```
P_CODE P_NAME           PRICE LAUNCH_DT
------ ---------------- ----- ---- ----
1      Nail             10.00 31-MAR-13
2      Washer           15.00 29-MAR-13
3      Nut              15.00 29-MAR-13
4      Screw            25.00 30-MAR-13
5      Super_Nut        30.00 30-MAR-13
6      New Nut           NULL      NULL
```

the query will return these rows.

```
P_CODE  P_NAME           PRICE_CAT
------  ---------------  ---------
1       Nail             Cheap
2       Washer           Medium
3       Nut              Medium
4       Screw            Expensive
6       New Nut          Others
5       Super_Nut        Others
```

The Searched CASE

The case in the Simple CASE compares a column with various values. On the hand, the case in the Searched CASE can be any condition. Here is the syntax for the Searched CASE.

```
SELECT columns,
  CASE
    WHEN condition1
    THEN output_value1
    WHEN condition2
    THEN output_value2
    WHEN ...
    ELSE else_value
  END AS output_column
FROM table
WHERE ... ;
```

The conditions are evaluated starting from the first WHEN and down to the last WHEN. If a WHEN condition is met, its THEN output_value is returned to the output_column and the CASE process stops. If none of the WHEN conditions is met, *else_value* is returned if there exists an ELSE clause. If no condition is met and no ELSE clause exists, NULL will be returned.

For instance, the query in Listing 3.8 uses a Searched CASE. While the Simple CASE in Listing 3.7 categorized the products based on only their prices, this Searched CASE categorizes the products based on the various conditions which can involve more than just the price. Note that in the Search CASE, NULL equality can be a condition, something that is not allowed in the Simple CASE.

Listing 3.8: An example of the Searched CASE

```
SELECT p_code,
  p_name,
  CASE
    WHEN (price <= 10
    AND p_name NOT LIKE 'Nut%')
    THEN 'Cheap'
    WHEN price BETWEEN 11 AND 25
    THEN 'Medium'
    WHEN price > 25 and TO_CHAR(launch_dt, 'YYYYMMDD') > '20130329'
    THEN 'Expensive'
    WHEN price IS NULL
    THEN 'Not valid'
```

```
    ELSE 'Others'
  END AS product_cat
FROM product;
```

Applying the query against the following product table

```
P_CODE  P_NAME           PRICE LAUNCH_DT
------  ---------------- ----- ---- ----
1       Nail             10.00 31-MAR-13
2       Washer           15.00 29-MAR-13
3       Nut              15.00 29-MAR-13
4       Screw            25.00 30-MAR-13
5       Super_Nut        30.00 30-MAR-13
6       New Nut          NULL      NULL
```

will return the following rows.

```
P_CODE  P_NAME           PRODUCT_CAT
------  ---------------- -----------
1       Nail             Cheap
2       Washer           Medium
3       Nut              Medium
4       Screw            Medium
5       Super_Nut        Expensive
6       New Nut          Not valid
```

Ordering Output Rows

To provide better visualization of the output, you can order output rows based on certain criteria. To order the output, use the ORDER BY clause. The ORDER BY clause must appear last in a SELECT statement.

Here is the syntax for a query having the ORDER BY clause.

```
SELECT columns FROM
table
WHERE condition ORDER BY column(s)
```

You can order output rows in one of the following methods.

- by one or more columns
- in ascending or descending direction
- by using the GROUP BY clause
- by using UNION and other set operators

Each of the methods is explained in the subsections below.

Ordering by One Column

To order your query output rows, use the ORDER BY clause with one column. For instance, have a look at the query in Listing 3.9.

Listing 3.9: Ordering by one column
```
SELECT * FROM product ORDER BY p_name;
```

When you apply the query against the following product table

```
P_CODE P_NAME           PRICE LAUNCH_DT
------ ---------------- ----- ---- ----
1      Nail             10.00 31-MAR-13
2      Washer           15.00 29-MAR-13
3      Nut              15.00 29-MAR-13
4      Screw            25.00 30-MAR-13
5      Super_Nut        30.00 30-MAR-13
6      New Nut          NULL       NULL
```

you will see the following output.

```
P_CODE P_NAME              PRICE LAUNCH_DT
------ ---------------- ---------- ---------
1      Nail                   10 31-MAR-13
6      New Nut              NULL       NULL
3      Nut                    15 29-MAR-13
4      Screw                  25 30-MAR-13
5      Super_Nut              30 30-MAR-13
2      Washer                 15 29-MAR-13
```

Direction of Order

The default direction is ascending. To order a column in descending direction, use the DESC reserved word. For example, the query in Listing 3.10 is similar to that in Listing 3.9 except that the output is presented in descending order.

Listing 3.10: Changing the order direction
```
SELECT * FROM product ORDER BY p_name DESC;
```

The output rows will be returned with p_name sorted in descending order.

```
P_CODE P_NAME              PRICE LAUNCH_DT
------ ---------------- ---------- ---------
2      Washer                 15 29-MAR-13
5      Super_Nut              30 30-MAR-13
4      Screw                  25 30-MAR-13
3      Nut                    15 29-MAR-13
6      New Nut            NULL       NULL
1      Nail                   10 31-MAR-13
```

Multiple Columns

To order by more than one column, list the columns in the ORDER BY clause. The sequence of columns listed is significant. The order will be conducted by the first column in the list, followed by the second column, and so on. For example, if the ORDER BY clause has two columns, the query output will first be ordered by the first column. Any rows with identical values in the first column will be further ordered by the second column.

For example, the query in Listing 3.11 uses an ORDER BY clause with two columns.

Listing 3.11: Multiple column ordering

```
SELECT * FROM product ORDER BY launch_dt, price;
```

Applying the query against the **product** table.

```
P_CODE P_NAME          PRICE LAUNCH_DT
------ ---------------- ----- ---- ----
1      Nail             10.00 31-MAR-13
2      Washer           15.00 29-MAR-13
3      Nut              15.00 29-MAR-13
4      Screw            25.00 30-MAR-13
5      Nut              30.00 30-MAR-13
6      Nut              NULL     NULL
```

The output rows will first be ordered by **launch_dt** and then by **price**, both in ascending order. The secondary ordering by **price** is seen on the Screw and Super_Nut rows. Their launch_dt's are the same, 30-MAR-13. Their prices are different, Screw's lower than Super_Nut's, hence Screw row comes before the Super_Nut.

```
P_CODE P_NAME       PRICE LAUNCH_DT
------ ---------- ------ ---------
3      Nut         15.00 29-MAR-13
2      Washer      15.00 29-MAR-13
4      Screw       25.00 30-MAR-13
5      Super_Nut   30.00 30-MAR-13
1      Nail        10.00 31-MAR-13
6      New Nut     NULL  NULL
```

Different Directions on Different Columns

You can apply different order directions on ordered columns too. For example, the query in Listing 3.12 uses different directions on different columns in its ORDER BY clause.

Listing 3.12: Using multiple directions of ORDER

```
SELECT * FROM product ORDER BY launch_dt, price DESC;
```

Applying the query against the **product** table, the output rows will be ordered by **launch_dt** in ascending order and then by **price** in descending order. Now, the Super_Nut comes before the Screw.

```
P_CODE P_NAME       PRICE LAUNCH_DT
------ ---------- ------ ---------
3      Nut         15.00 29-MAR-13
2      Washer      15.00 29-MAR-13
5      Super_Nut   30.00 30-MAR-13
4      Screw       25.00 30-MAR-13
1      Nail        10.00 31-MAR-13
6      New Nut     NULL  NULL
```

Ordering with a WHERE clause

If your SELECT statement has both the WHERE clause and the ORDER BY clause, ORDER BY must appear after the WHERE clause.

For example, the query in Listing 3.13 has both WHERE and ORDER BY. This query will return only Nut products.

Listing 3.13: Using both WHERE and ORDER BY

```
SELECT * FROM product WHERE p_name = 'Nut'
ORDER BY p_name, p_code DESC;
```

If you execute the query, you will see one row only, the Nut, in the output window.

```
P_CODE P_NAME      PRICE LAUNCH_DT
------ ---------- ------ ---------
3      Nut        15.00 29-MAR-13
```

Storing Query Output

You can store a query output into a new or existing table. To store a query output in a new table, use the following statement:

```
CREATE TABLE new_table AS SELECT ... ;
```

For instance, the query in Listing 3.14 executes a SELECT statement and stores its result in a new table called nut_product.

Listing 3.14: Storing output into a new table

```
CREATE TABLE nut_product AS
SELECT * FROM product WHERE p_name LIKE '%Nut%';
```

Applied against the **product** table, the query in Listing 3.14 will create a **nut_product** table with the following content.

```
P_CODE P_NAME           PRICE LAUNCH_DT
------ ---------------- ------ ---------
3      Nut                 15 29-MAR-13
6      New Nut           NULL NULL
5      Super_Nut           30 30-MAR-13
```

To store a query output into an existing table, use this syntax.

```
INSERT INTO existing_table AS SELECT ... ;
```

For example, the query in Listing 3.15 stores the query result in an existing table.

Listing 3.15: Storing output into an existing table

```
INSERT INTO non_nut
SELECT * FROM product WHERE p_name NOT LIKE '%Nut%';
```

Before executing INSERT statement of Listing 3.15, first you have to create a **non_nut** table by executing the following statement.

```
CREATE TABLE non_nut
  (
    p_code      VARCHAR2(6),
    p_name      VARCHAR2(15),
    price       NUMBER(4,2),
    launch_dt DATE,
    PRIMARY KEY (p_code)
  );
```

Applying the query in Listing 3.15 against this **product** table

```
P_CODE P_NAME            PRICE LAUNCH_DT
------ --------------- ------ ---------
1      Nail               10 31-MAR-13
2      Washer             15 29-MAR-13
3      Nut                15 29-MAR-13
4      Screw              25 30-MAR-13
6      New Nut          NULL   NULL
5      Super_Nut          30 30-MAR-13
```

you will get a **non_nut** table containing the following rows.

```
P_CODE P_NAME            PRICE LAUNCH_DT
------ --------------- ------ ---------
1      Nail               10 31-MAR-13
2      Washer             15 29-MAR-13
4      Screw              25 30-MAR-13
```

Summary

SQL allows you to retrieve rows from a table and manipulate the output. You learned in this chapter that you can create aliases, use aggregate functions, and order rows.

Chapter 4
Grouping

A group is a set of rows having the same value on specific columns. In Chapter 3, "Query Output" you learned how to apply aggregate functions on all output rows. In this chapter you will learn how to create groups and apply aggregate functions on those groups.

The GROUP BY Clause

In a query the GROUP BY clause appears after the WHERE clause and before the ORDER clause, if any. Here is the syntax for a SELECT statement with the WHERE, GROUP BY, and ORDER BY clauses.

```
SELECT columns,
  aggregate_function(group_columns)
FROM table(s)
WHERE condition
GROUP BY group_columns
ORDER BY column(s);
```

As an example, the query in Listing 4.1 groups the output from the **product** table by the launch date.

Listing 4.1: Grouping on one column

```
SELECT launch_dt,
  MAX(price) MAX,
  MIN(price) MIN,
  SUM(price) SUM,
  AVG(price) AVG,
  COUNT(price) COUNT,
  COUNT(*) AS "COUNT(*)"
FROM product
GROUP BY launch_dt
ORDER BY launch_dt;
```

Applied against a **product** table with the following rows, aggregations will be done by the four grouped launch dates: 29, 30 and 31 of March 2013, and NULL.

```
P_CODE P_NAME           PRICE LAUNCH_DT
------ ---------------- ----- ---- ----
1      Nail             10.00 31-MAR-13
```

```
2       Washer          15.00 29-MAR-13
3       Nut             15.00 29-MAR-13
4       Screw           25.00 30-MAR-13
5       Super_Nut       30.00 30-MAR-13
6       New Nut         NULL  NULL
```

The query output will have four rows, one for each of the four grouped launch dates. Note that the COUNT(price) element, which counts the rows with a value on their price column, produces 0. On the other hand, the COUNT(*) element, which counts the NULL launch dates, produces 1.

LAUNCH_DT	MAX	MIN	SUM	AVG	COUNT	COUNT(*)
29-MAR-13	15	15	30	15	2	2
30-MAR-13	30	25	55	27.5	2	2
31-MAR-13	10	10	10	10	1	1
NULL	NULL	NULL	NULL	NULL	0	1

You can group rows by more than one column. If you do that, rows having the same value on all the columns will form a group. As an example, the query in Listing 4.2 groups rows by price and launch date.

Listing 4.2: Grouping on two columns

```
SELECT price,
  launch_dt,
  MAX(price) MAX,
  MIN(price) MIN,
  SUM(price) SUM,
  AVG(price) AVG,
  COUNT(price) COUNT,
  COUNT(*) "COUNT(*)"
FROM product
GROUP BY price,
  launch_dt
ORDER BY price,
  launch_dt;
```

Applied to the same **product** table, the output will have five rows. Even though the Screw and Super_Nut have the same price, they have different launch dates, and therefore form different groups.

PRICE	LAUNCH_DT	MAX	MIN	SUM	AVG	COUNT	COUNT(*)
10	31-MAR-13	10	10	10	10	1	1
15	29-MAR-13	15	15	30	15	2	2
25	30-MAR-13	25	25	25	25	1	1
30	30-MAR-13	30	30	30	30	1	1
NULL	NULL	NULL	NULL	NULL	NULL	0	1

The HAVING Keyword

The WHERE condition can be used to select individual rows. On the other hand, the HAVING condition is used for selecting individual groups. Only groups that satisfy the condition in the HAVING clause will be returned by the query. In other words, the HAVING condition is on the aggregate, not on a column.

If present, the HAVING clause must appear after the GROUP BY, as in the following syntax.

```
SELECT columns,
   aggregate_function(group_columns)
FROM table(s)
WHERE condition
GROUP BY group_columns
HAVING aggregate_condition
ORDER BY columns;
```

As an example, the query in Listing 4.3 uses the HAVING condition.

Listing 4.3: Using the HAVING condition
```
SELECT price,
   launch_dt,
   MAX(price) MAX,
   MIN(price) MIN,
   SUM(price) SUM,
   AVG(price) AVG,
   COUNT(price) COUNT,
   COUNT(*) "COUNT(*)"
FROM product
GROUP BY price,
   launch_dt
HAVING COUNT(price) > 1
ORDER BY price,
   launch_dt;
```

Only groups having more than one row (satisfying the COUNT(price) > 1 condition) will be returned. Only one row will be returned, the one with price = 15 and launch date = 29-MAR-13.

PRICE	LAUNCH_DT	MAX	MIN	SUM	AVG	COUNT	COUNT(*)
15	29-MAR-13	15	15	30	15	2	2

If a WHERE clause is present, it must appear after the GROUP BY clause. Individual rows will be selected by the WHERE condition first before grouping occurs. For instance, the query in Listing 4.4 uses both WHERE and GROUP BY.

Listing 4.4: Grouping with WHERE
```
SELECT launch_dt,
   MAX(price) MAX,
```

```
  MIN(price) MIN,
  SUM(price) SUM,
  AVG(price) AVG,
  COUNT(price) COUNT,
  COUNT(*) "COUNT(*)"
FROM product
WHERE p_name NOT LIKE 'Super%'
GROUP BY launch_dt
HAVING launch_dt > '29-MAR-13'
ORDER BY launch_dt;
```

Here is the query output.

```
LAUNCH_DT  MAX    MIN    SUM    AVG    COUNT   COUNT(*)
---------  -----  -----  -----  -----  ------  ----------
30-MAR-13  25.0   25.0   25.0   25.0      1           1
31-MAR-13  10.0   10.0   10.0   10.0      1           1
```

In this case, Super_Nut does not satisfy the WHERE condition. As such, it is not included in the aggregation.

Applying aggregate as a WHERE condition clause is not allowed. This is shown in Listing 4.5, which contains a query that throws an error if executed.

Listing 4.5: Error with WHERE on the aggregate

```
SELECT price,
  launch_dt,
  MAX(price) MAX,
  MIN(price) MIN,
  SUM(price) SUM,
  AVG(price) AVG,
  COUNT(price) COUNT,
  COUNT(*) "COUNT(*)"
FROM product
WHERE COUNT(price) > 1;
```

Executing this query will give you this error message.

```
ORA-00934: group function is not allowed here
```

Summary

In this chapter you learned how to aggregate values from rows. You also learned to use the HAVING condition applied on aggregates. In the next chapter you will learn about the JOIN clause used to "aggregate" rows from more than one table.

Chapter 5
Joins

A real-world database typically stores data in dozens or even hundreds of tables. In these multi-table databases, a table often relates to one or some other tables. In this environment, you should be able to relate rows from two or more tables by using the JOIN clause. This chapter shows you how.

Primary Keys and Foreign Keys

In Chapter 1, "Storing and Maintaining Data" you learned about primary keys. A primary key is a column, or a set of columns, which uniquely identifies every row in a table. A foreign key is a column, or a set of columns, which is used to relate to the primary key of another table. The process of using the foreign key/primary key to relate rows from two tables is called joining.

While a primary key must be unique, a foreign key does not have to be unique. You can have a foreign key in more than one row. For example, in a **customer order** table you can have many orders for the same product. In this **customer order** table, a product is represented by its foreign key, e.g. **product code**, which is the primary key of the **product** table.

Even though the use of primary and foreign keys is not an absolute requirement for joining tables, their absence may cause you to incorrectly join tables.

Querying Multiple Tables

To query data from multiple tables, use the JOIN keyword to specify the related columns from two tables. The JOIN clause of a SELECT statement joins related rows from two or more tables, based on their primary key/foreign key relationship.

For example, a **customer order (c_order)** table may need a foreign key column to relate to the primary key of the **product** table. Additionally, the **customer order** table may also need a foreign key to relate to the primary key of the **customer** table.

The syntax for the JOIN is as follows.

```
SELECT columns FROM table_1, table_2, ... table_n
WHERE table_1.primary_key = table_2.foreign_key
```

```
AND table_2.primary_key = table_n.foregin_key;
```

To illustrate the use of joins, I will use the **c_order**, **customer**, and **product** tables in Table 5.1, Table 5.2, and Table 5.3, respectively. The **C_NO** and **P_CODE** columns in the **c_order** table are foreign keys; their related primary keys are in the **customer** and **product** tables, respectively.

```
C_NO P_CODE  QTY ORDER_DT
---- ------ ---- ---------
  10  1      100 01-APR-13
  10  2      100 01-APR-13
  20  1      200 01-APR-13
  30  3      300 02-APR-13
  40  4      400 02-APR-13
  40  5      400 03-APR-13
```

Table 5.1: The customer order (c_order) table

```
C_NO C_NAME
---- --------------
  10 Standard Store
  20 Quality Store
  30 Head Office
  40 Super Agent
```

Table 5.2: The customer table

```
P_CODE P_NAME           PRICE LAUNCH_DT
------ --------------- ----- ---- ----
1      Nail            10.00 31-MAR-13
2      Washer          15.00 29-MAR-13
3      Nut             15.00 29-MAR-13
4      Screw           25.00 30-MAR-13
5      Super_Nut       30.00 30-MAR-13
6      New Nut         NULL  NULL
```

Table 5.3: The product table

Listing 5.1 is an example of a JOIN query. It joins the rows from the **c_order** table to the rows from the **customer** table based on the **c_no** foreign key column of the **c_order** table and the **c_no** primary key column of the **customer** table. The query returns the name of every customer who has placed one or more orders.

Listing 5.1: A two table join

```
SELECT c_name,
  p_code,
  c_order.qty,
  c_order.order_dt
FROM c_order
JOIN customer
ON c_order.c_no = customer.c_no;
```

Applied against the example **c_order** and **customer** tables, the query result is as follows.

```
C_NAME                    P_CO      QTY ORDER_DT
------------------------- ---- ---------- ---------
Standard Store            2         100 01-APR-13
```

```
Standard Store          1          100 01-APR-13
Quality Store           1          200 01-APR-13
Head Office             3          300 02-APR-13
Super Agent             5          400 03-APR-13
Super Agent             4          400 02-APR-13
```

Using Table Aliases

In a join query, different tables can have columns with identical names. To make sure you refer to the correct column of a table, you need to qualify it with its table. In the previous example, **c_order.c_no** (the **c_no column** of the **c_order** table) and **customer.c_no** (the **c_no** column of the **customer** table) were how the **c_no columns** were qualified. A table alias can be a more convenient (and shorter) way to qualify a column.

For example, in the query in Listing 5.2, **o** is an alias for the **c_order** table and **c** is an alias for the **customer** table. These aliases are then used in the ON clause to qualify the **c_no** columns with their respective tables.

Listing 5.2: Using table aliases
```
SELECT c_name,
  p_code,
  o.qty,
  o.order_dt
FROM c_order o
JOIN customer c
ON o.c_no = c.c_no;
```

Column Aliases vs. Table Aliases
In Chapter 3, "Query Output", I explained the use of aliases for columns using the AS keyword. Although a column alias can be created without using the AS keyword, its presence improves readability ("p_name AS product_name" instead of "p_name product_name"). On the other hand, table aliases cannot use the AS keyword.

Joining More Than Two Tables

From the JOIN syntax presented earlier, you can join more than two tables. To do this, in the SELECT statement, join two tables at a time.

For example, the query in Listing 5.3 joins the **c_order** table to the **customer** table, and then joins the **customer** table to the **product** table. The rows in the **c_order** table are joined to the rows of the same **c_no** column from the **customer** table, and these rows are then joined to the rows with the same **p_code** from the **product** table. This query returns the customer names and their orders.

Listing 5.3: A three table join
```
SELECT c_name,
  p_name,
  o.qty,
```

```
   o.order_dt
FROM c_order o
JOIN customer c
ON o.c_no = c.c_no
JOIN product p
ON o.p_code = p.p_code;
```

Applied against the **c_order**, **customer** and **product** sample tables, you will see the following result.

```
C_NAME          P_NAME      QTY ORDER_DT
--------------- ----------  ---- ---------
Standard Store  Washer      100 01-APR-13
Standard Store  Nail        100 01-APR-13
Quality Store   Nail        200 01-APR-13
Head Office     Nut         300 02-APR-13
Super Agent     Super_nut   400 03-APR-13
Super Agent     Screw       400 02-APR-13
```

You can also apply WHERE conditions for selecting rows on a join query. For example, in Listing 5.4, thanks to the WHERE condition, only products with names that do not start with "Super" will be in the query output.

Listing 5.4: JOIN and WHERE

```
SELECT c_name,
  p_name,
  o.qty,
  o.order_dt
FROM c_order o
JOIN customer c
ON o.c_no = c.c_no
JOIN product p
ON o.p_code = p.p_code
WHERE p_name NOT LIKE 'Super%';
```

Executing the query in Listing 5.4 against the sample tables will produce the following output rows.

```
C_NAME          P_NAME      QTY ORDER_DT
--------------- ----------  ---- ---------
Standard Store  Washer      100 01-APR-13
Standard Store  Nail        100 01-APR-13
Quality Store   Nail        200 01-APR-13
Branch Office   Nut         300 02-APR-13
Super Agent     Screw       400 02-APR-13
```

Joining on More than One Column

The preceding joins were on one column. Tables can also be joined on more than one column.

The syntax for a multicolumn join for two tables is as follows.

```
SELECT columns FROM table_1, table_2
```

```
WHERE table_1.column_1 = table_2.column_1
AND table_1.column_2 = table_2.column_2
...
AND table_1.column_n = table_2.column_n;
```

As an example, suppose you track order shipments in the following **shipment** table

C_NO	P_CODE	ORDER_DT	SHIP_QTY	SHIP_DT
10	1	01-APR-13	50	02-APR-13
10	2	01-APR-13	100	02-APR-13
20	1	01-APR-13	100	02-APR-13
30	3	02-APR-13	300	03-APR-13
10	1	01-APR-13	50	10-APR-13

To retrieve the order quantity (the **qty** column of the **c_order** table) of each shipment, you need to have a query that joins the **shipment** table to the **order** table on three columns, **c_no**, **p_no**, and **order_dt**, as shown in the query in Listing 5.5.

Listing 5.5: A multiple columns join

```
SELECT o.c_no,
   o.p_code,
   o.order_dt,
   ship_qty,
   ship_dt,
   qty
FROM shipment s
JOIN c_order o
ON s.c_no     = o.c_no
AND s.p_code  = o.p_code
AND s.order_dt = o.order_dt;
```

Executing this query against the **c_order** and **shipment** tables will give you the following output rows.

C_NO	P_CODE	ORDER_DT	SHIP_QTY	SHIP_DT	QTY
10	1	01-APR-13	50	10-APR-13	100
10	1	01-APR-13	50	02-APR-13	100
10	2	01-APR-13	100	02-APR-13	100
20	1	01-APR-13	100	02-APR-13	200
30	3	02-APR-13	300	03-APR-13	300

Outer Joins

All the joins I explained so far were inner joins. There is another type of join, the outer join. While an inner join query produces only related rows from the joined tables, an outer join query produces all rows from one table even when some of the rows do not have matching rows from the other table.

There are three subtypes of outer joins, LEFT, RIGHT, and FULL. The following points described each of these three types.

All rows from the table on the left of the left outer join will be in the output whether or not there are matching rows from the table on its right. The syntax for the left outer join is as follows.

```
SELECT columns
FROM table_1 LEFT OUTER JOIN table_2
ON table_1.column = table_2.column ... ;
```

All rows form the table on the right of the right outer join will be in the output whether or not there are matching rows from the table on its left. The syntax for the right outer join is as follows.

```
SELECT columns FROM table_1 RIGHT OUTER JOIN table_2 ON table_1.column =
        table_2.column ... ;
```

The full outer join returns all rows from both tables whether or not there are matching rows from the opposite table. The syntax for the full outer join is as follows.

```
SELECT columns
FROM table_1 FULL OUTER JOIN table_2
ON table_1.column = table_2.column … ;
```

Listing 5.6 is an example left outer join query. This query returns all rows from the c_order table.

Listing 5.6: Left outer join

```
SELECT o.*,
  ship_dt
FROM c_order o
LEFT OUTER JOIN shipment s
ON o.p_code = s.p_code
AND o.c_no  = s.c_no;
```

If you run this query against our example **c_order** and **shipment** tables, you will see the following output rows.

```
C_NO P_CODE       QTY ORDER_DT  SHIP_DT
---- ------ ---------- --------- ---------
10   1          100 01-APR-13 02-APR-13
10   2          100 01-APR-13 02-APR-13
20   1          200 01-APR-13 02-APR-13
30   3          300 02-APR-13 03-APR-13
10   1          100 01-APR-13 10-APR-13
40   4          400 02-APR-13 NULL
40   5          400 03-APR-13 NULL
```

Note that the last two rows have no matching rows from the shipment table and therefore their ship_dt column has NULL values.

Rows with NULL only

If you want to query only orders that have not been shipped at all, you have to put this "only" condition in the WHERE clause of your query (ship_dt IS NULL) as in the query in Listing 5.7.

Listing 5.7: NULL only rows

```
SELECT o.*,
  ship_dt
FROM c_order o
LEFT OUTER JOIN shipment s
ON o.p_code = s.p_code
AND o.c_no  = s.c_no
WHERE s.ship_dt IS NULL;
```

The following output rows from the query in Listing 5.7 are customer orders that have not been shipped.

```
C_NO P_CODE        QTY ORDER_DT  SHIP_DT
---- ------ ---------- --------- ---------
40   4             400 02-APR-13 NULL
40   5             400 03-APR-13 NULL
```

Full Outer Joins

Suppose any order that was canceled was deleted from the **c_order** table (In a real-life application, canceled orders might be moved to a different table, rather than deleted). This means, some rows of the shipment table now may not have matching rows in the order table. To return orders that do not have shipments as well shipments that do not have orders, we need to write a query with the full outer join, like the one shown in Listing 5.8.

Listing 5.8: Full outer join

```
SELECT o.*, s.*
  FROM c_order o
FULL OUTER JOIN shipment s
ON o.p_code = s.p_code
AND o.c_no  = s.c_no ;
```

To test the query, you need delete an order, such as the order(s) placed by customer 30. After the deletion, the **c_order** table has the following rows.

```
C_NO P_CODE        QTY ORDER_DT
---- ------ ---------- ---------
10   1             100 01-APR-13
10   2             100 01-APR-13
20   1             200 01-APR-13
40   4             400 02-APR-13
40   5             400 03-APR-13
```

If you run the query in Listing 5.8, you will get the following output rows. Note that we have NULL on the rows on both sides. The NULLs on the right side are from the shipment table, the NULL on the left side (in our example here we only have one row) is coming from the **c_order** table.

```
C_NO P_CO  QTY  ORDER_DT  C_NO P_CO ORDER_DT    SHIP_QTY SHIP_DT
---- ----  ----- --------- ---- ---- --------- ----------- ---------
10   1     100  01-APR-13 10   1    01-APR-13         50 02-APR-13
10   2     100  01-APR-13 10   2    01-APR-13        100 02-APR-13
20   1     200  01-APR-13 20   1    01-APR-13        100 02-APR-13
```

```
10   1      100   01-APR-13 10    1     01-APR-13           50 10-APR-13
40   4      400   02-APR-13 NULL NULL NULL        NULL     NULL
40   5      400   03-APR-13 NULL NULL NULL        NULL     NULL
NULL NULL   NULL NULL       30    3     02-APR-13          300 03-APR-13
```

Self-Joins

Assuming some of your products have substitutes and you want to record the substitutes in the **product** table, you then need to add a column. The new column, which is called **s_code** in the **product** table, contains the product code of the substitute.

The new **product** table, with a row having **s_code** 5, now looks like the following.

```
P_CODE P_NAME              PRICE LAUNCH_DT S_CODE
------ --------------- ---------- --------- ------
1       Nail                10 31-MAR-13 NULL
2       Washer              15 29-MAR-13 NULL
3       Nut                 15 29-MAR-13 5
4       Screw               25 30-MAR-13 NULL
5       Super_Nut           30 30-MAR-13 NULL
6       New Nut           NULL NULL        NULL
```

To add the **s_code** column, execute the following statement:

```
ALTER TABLE product ADD (s_code VARCHAR2(6));
```

Then, to update rows with p_code = 3, execute the following statement:

```
UPDATE product SET s_code = 5 WHERE p_code = 3;
```

If you need to know the product name of a substitute, you need the query shown in Listing 5.9. This query joins the **product** table to itself. This kind of join is called a self-join.

The syntax for the self-join is as follows.

```
SELECT columns
FROM table alias_1
JOIN table alias_2
ON alias_1.column_x = alias_2.column_y;
```

Note that *column_x* and *column_y* are columns in the same table.

Listing 5.9: A self-join
```
SELECT prod.p_code,
   prod.p_name,
   subst.p_code subst_p_code,
   subst.p_name subst_name
FROM product prod
LEFT OUTER JOIN product subst
ON prod.s_code = subst.p_code
ORDER BY prod.p_code;
```

Here are the output rows of the query, showing "Newer Nut" in the subst_name column of the third row.

```
P_CODE P_NAME      SUBST_  SUBST_NAME
------ ----------  ------  ----------
1      Nail        NULL    NULL
2      Washer      NULL    NULL
3      Nut         5       Super_Nut
4      Screw       NULL    NULL
5      Super_Nut   NULL    NULL
6      New Nut     NULL    NULL
```

Multiple Uses of A Table

If a product can have more than one substitute, you need to store the product-substitute relationships in a separate table. A substitute cannot be recorded in the **product** table.

To create a table that stores the product-substitute relationships named **prod_subst**, execute the following statement.

```
CREATE TABLE prod_subst (p_code VARCHAR2(6), s_code VARCHAR2(6));
```

To remove the **s_code** column, execute this statement:

```
ALTER TABLE product DROP (s_code);
```

Your **product** table will now contain the following rows.

```
P_CODE P_NAME           PRICE LAUNCH_DT
------ --------------- ----------- ---------
1      Nail              10 31-MAR-13
2      Washer            15 29-MAR-13
3      Nut               15 29-MAR-13
4      Screw             25 30-MAR-13
5      Super_Nut         30 30-MAR-13
6      New Nut         NULL NULL
```

Assuming that the only product with substitutes is product number 3 and its substitutes are the products numbered 5 and 6, the **prod_subst** table will have two rows as follows. (You need to insert these two rows using the INSERT statements)

```
P_NO SUBS_CODE
---- ---------
3    5
3    6
```

To get the name of a product and the names of its substitutes, you need to use the **product** table twice, as shown in the query in Listing 5.10.

Listing 5.10: Multiple uses of a table
```
SELECT prod.p_code,
  prod.p_name,
  ps.s_code,
  subst.p_name AS s_name
```

```
FROM product prod
INNER JOIN prod_subst ps
ON prod.p_code = ps.p_code
INNER JOIN product subst
ON ps.s_code = subst.p_code
ORDER BY prod.p_code;
```

Here are the output rows from the query in Listing 5.10.

```
P_CODE P_NAME    S_CODE S_NAME
------ --------- ------ ---------
3      Nut       6      Newer_Nut
3      Nut       5      Super_Nut
```

Natural Joins

If two tables have columns that share a name, you can naturally join the two tables on these columns. In a natural join, you do not need to specify the columns that the join should use.

The syntax for the natural join is this.

```
SELECT columns FROM table_1 NATURAL JOIN table_2 ... ;
```

Listing 5.11 shows an example of a natural join on the **c_order** and **customer** tables. This natural join implicitly joins the tables on their **c_no** columns.

Listing 5.11: A natural join

```
SELECT * FROM c_order NATURAL JOIN customer;
```

Running the query in Listing 5.11 gives you the following output rows.

```
C_NO P_CO QTY  ORDER_DT   C_NAME
---- ---- ---- ---------- --------------
10   1    100  01-APR-13  Standard Store
10   2    100  01-APR-13  Standard Store
20   1    200  01-APR-13  Quality Store
40   4    400  02-APR-13  Super Agent
40   5    400  03-APR-13  Super Agent
```

Natural Outer Joins

The natural join is also applicable to the outer join. Consider the query in Listing 5.12.

Listing 5.12: A natural outer join

```
SELECT * FROM c_order NATURAL RIGHT JOIN customer;
```

Applying the query against the **c_order** and **customer** tables will give you the following output rows.

```
C_NO P_CODE        QTY ORDER_DT  C_NAME
---- ------ ---------- --------- --------------
  10 1             100 01-APR-13 Standard Store
  10 2             100 01-APR-13 Standard Store
  20 1             200 01-APR-13 Quality Store
  40 4             400 02-APR-13 Super Agent
  40 5             400 03-APR-13 Super Agent
  30 NULL        NULL NULL       Head Office
```

Mixing Natural Joins with Different Column Names

If you need to join on more than one column, and the second column pair does not share a name, you can specify the different column names in the WHERE clause. Listing 5.13 shows an example of such a case.

Listing 5.13: Mixing natural join with different column names
```
SELECT * FROM c_order o NATURAL RIGHT JOIN product p
WHERE o.order_dt = p.launch_dt;
```

In the query in Listing 5.13, in addition to the natural join on the same **c_no** column, the rows from the two tables have to be joined on the two dates.

The query does not return any row as we don't have any order of a product with the same order date as the product's launch date.

The USING Keyword

A natural join uses all columns with the same names from the joined tables. If you want your query to join only on some of these identically named columns, instead of using the NATURAL keyword, use the USING keyword.

The syntax for joining two tables with USING is as follows.

```
SELECT columns
FROM table_1
JOIN table_2 USING (column);
```

Listing 5.14, for example, joins the **c_order** table to the **shipment** table only on their **p_code** columns. It does not join the tables on their **c_no** columns. This query gives you the total quantity shipped by product code.

Listing 5.14: USING
```
SELECT p_code,
  SUM(s.ship_qty)
FROM c_order o
JOIN shipment s USING (p_code)
GROUP BY p_code;
```

Executing this query against our example **c_order** and **shipment** tables will produce the following output rows.

```
P_CODE SUM(S.SHIP_QTY)
------ ---------------
1                  400
2                  100
```

Summary

In this chapter you learned about getting data from multiple tables. You learned how to use the various types of joins for this purpose.

Chapter 6
Subqueries

A subquery is a query nested within another query. The containing query is called an outer query. A subquery in turn can have a nested query, making it a multiply nested query.

This chapter discusses subqueries in detail.

Single-Row Subqueries

A single-row subquery is a subquery that returns a single value. A single-row subquery can be placed in the WHERE clause of an outer query. The return value of the subquery is compared with a column of the outer query using one of the comparison operators. (Comparison operators were discussed in Chapter 2, "Basic Queries")

For example, the query in Listing 6.1 contains a single-row subquery that returns the highest sale price recorded for a product. The outer query returns all products from the **product** table that have that highest price (30.00), the Super_Nut and Newer Nut products.

Listing 6.1: A subquery that returns a single value

```
SELECT *
FROM product
WHERE price =
  (SELECT MAX(price)
  FROM product p
  INNER JOIN c_order o
  ON p.p_code = o.p_code
  );
```

Note that the subquery in Listing 6.1 is printed in bold.

Executing the query in Listing 6.1 against this **product** table

```
P_CODE P_NAME      PRICE LAUNCH_DT
------ ----------- ----- ---------
1      Nail        10.00 31-MAR-13
2      Washer      15.00 29-MAR-13
3      Nut         15.00 29-MAR-13
4      Screw       25.00 30-MAR-13
5      Super_Nut   30.00 30-MAR-13
6      Newer_Nut   30.00 01-MAY-13
```

and the following **c_order** (customer order) table

```
C_NO P_CODE  QTY ORDER_DT
---- ------ ---- ---------
10   1       100 01-APR-13
10   2       100 01-APR-13
20   1       200 01-APR-13
30   3       300 02-APR-13
40   4       400 02-APR-13
40   5       400 03-APR-13
```

will give you the following result.

```
P_CODE P_NAME       PRICE LAUNCH_DT
------ ---------- ------ ---------
5      Super_Nut   30.00 30-MAR-13
6      Newer_Nut   30.00 01-MAY-13
```

The column and subquery result do not have to be the same column, but they must have compatible data types. In the query in Listing 6.1, the **price** column of the **product** table is a numeric type and the subquery also returns a numeric type.

If the subquery returns more than one value, you will get an error message. For example, the query in Listing 6.2 throws an error because the subquery returns more than one value.

Listing 6.2: Single-row subquery error
```
SELECT *
FROM product
WHERE price =
  (SELECT MAX(price)
  FROM product p
  INNER JOIN c_order s
  ON p.p_code = s.p_code
  GROUP BY p.launch_dt
  );
```

Here is the error that you will see if you run the query in Listing 6.2.

```
ERROR at line 4:
ORA-01427: single-row subquery returns more than one row
```

Multiple-Row Subqueries

A subquery that returns more than one value is called a multiple-row subquery. This type of subquery also occurs in the WHERE clause of an outer query, however instead of using a comparison operator, you use IN or NOT IN in the WHERE clause.

For example, the query in Listing 6.3 contains a multiple-row subquery.

Listing 6.3: Using a multiple-row subquery
```
SELECT *
```

```
FROM product
WHERE price IN
   (SELECT MAX(price)
   FROM product p
   INNER JOIN c_order s
   ON p.p_code = s.p_code
   GROUP BY p.launch_dt
   );
```

Run against the same **product** and **order** tables, the subquery will return these three values:

```
MAX(PRICE)
----------
        15
        30
        10
```

The overall query output will be as follows.

```
P_CODE P_NAME       PRICE LAUNCH_DT
------ ----------   ------ ---------
1      Nail         10.00 31-MAR-13
2      Washer       15.00 29-MAR-13
3      Nut          15.00 29-MAR-13
5      Super_Nut    30.00 30-MAR-13
6      Newer_Nut    30.00 01-MAY-13
```

The ALL and ANY Operators

In addition to IN and NOT IN, you can also use the ALL and ANY operators in a multiple-row subquery. With ALL or ANY you use a comparison operator. For instance, the query in Listing 6.4 uses the ALL operator to compare the **price** column with the subquery result.

Listing 6.4: Using ALL
```
SELECT *
FROM product
WHERE price >= ALL
   (SELECT MAX(price)
   FROM product p
   INNER JOIN c_order o
   ON o.p_code = o.p_code
   GROUP BY p.launch_dt
   )
ORDER BY p_code;
```

Run against the same **product** and **order** tables, the subquery in Listing 6.4 (printed in bold) returns these results:

```
MAX(PRICE)
----------
        15
        30
```

```
10
```

The query output will consist of only rows whose price is greater or equal to all the values returned by the subquery.

Here is the query output.

```
P_CODE P_NAME         PRICE LAUNCH_DT
------ ----------     ------ ---------
5       Super_Nut     30.00 30-MAR-13
6       Newer_Nut     30.00 01-MAY-13
```

As another example, the query in Listing 6.5 is similar to the one in Listing 6.4 except that the equal operator is used to compare the price with the subquery result.

Listing 6.5: Using ALL for equal comparison

```
SELECT *
FROM product
WHERE price = ALL
  (SELECT MAX(price)
  FROM product p
  INNER JOIN c_order o
  ON o.p_code = o.p_code
  GROUP BY p.launch_dt
  )
ORDER BY p_code;
```

As in the previous example, the subquery will return these values.

```
MAX(PRICE)
----------
        15
        30
        10
```

The query output then consists of only rows whose price equals to all these values, which is not possible as each product has only one price. As a result, the query returns no rows. Here is a message you will see if you run the query.

```
no rows selected
```

Subqueries Returning Rows Having the Same Value

If you use = ALL and the subquery returns one row or multiple rows with the same value you will not get a "no rows selected" message.

You can also use the ANY operator to compare a column with the values returned by a subquery. If you use ALL, the query compares a column to all values (every one of the values) returned by the subquery. If you use ANY, the query compares a column to any one of the values returned by the subquery.

For example, the query in Listing 6.6 compares the **price** column for equality to any of the maximum prices returned by the subquery, in other words, the WHERE condition is true if the price equals to any of maximum prices.

Listing 6.6: Using the equal comparison to ANY value

```
SELECT *
FROM product
WHERE price = ANY
  (SELECT MAX(price)
  FROM product p
  INNER JOIN c_order o
  ON p.P_code = o.p_code
  GROUP BY p.launch_dt
  )
ORDER BY p_code;
```

The subquery will return these rows.

```
MAX(PRICE)
----------
        15
        30
        10
```

The outer query output will consist of any product that has a price equal to any of these (maximum price) values. Here is the query output.

```
P_CODE  P_NAME       PRICE  LAUNCH_DT
------  ----------   ------ ---------
1       Nail         10.00  31-MAR-13
2       Washer       15.00  29-MAR-13
3       Nut          15.00  29-MAR-13
5       Super_Nut    30.00  30-MAR-13
6       Newer_Nut    30.00  01-MAY-13
```

Multiply Nested Subqueries

A subquery can contain another query, making the containing query a query with multiply nested subqueries. The query in Listing 6.7, for example, has multiply nested subqueries. Notice the two IN's, one for each of the two nested queries? The query returns only customers who have not ordered any product having name that contains 'Nut'.

Listing 6.7: Query with multiple nested subqueries

```
SELECT customer.*
FROM customer
WHERE c_no IN
  (SELECT c_no
  FROM c_order
  WHERE p_code IN
    (SELECT p_code FROM product WHERE p_name NOT LIKE '%Nut%'
    )
  );
```

ɛ is the query result.

```
 NO C_NAME
---- --------------
 40    Super Agent
 10    Standard Store
 20    Quality Store
```

Correlated Subqueries

All the preceding subqueries are independent of their outer queries. A subquery can also be related to its outer query, where one or more column from the outer query table is (are) related to the column(s) of the subquery table in the WHERE clause of the subquery. This type of subquery is called the correlated subquery.

As an example, the query in Listing 6.8 contains a correlated subquery that returns only customers who have not ordered any product whose name contains 'Nut'. Note that the **c_no** column of the outer query table, **customer**, is related to the **c_no** column of the **c_order** table of the subquery.

Listing 6.8: Using a correlated subquery

```
SELECT customer.*
FROM customer
WHERE c_no IN
  (SELECT c_no
   FROM c_order o
   JOIN product p
   ON o.p_code = p.p_code
   WHERE p_name NOT LIKE '%Nut%'
   AND customer.c_no = o.c_no
   );
```

The following are the query result.

```
C_NO C_NAME
---- --------------
 40    Super Agent
 10    Standard Store
 20    Quality Store
```

Factoring

Using a WITH clause you can factor out a subquery placing it above the main SELECT, and give it a name. You can then use it in the main query by referring its name as if it is a table.

Here is the syntax of the WITH clause.

```
WITH sub_query_name AS (subquery)
SELECT ...
```

```
);
```

I will use the previous example in Listing 6.1 to show a subquery factoring. Here is Listing 6.1 for your reference.

```
SELECT *
FROM product
WHERE price =
  (SELECT MAX(price)
  FROM product p
  INNER JOIN c_order o
  ON p.p_code = o.p_code
    );
```

The following Listing 6.9 factors out the subquery.

Listing 6.9: Factoring a subquery

```
WITH max_price AS
  (SELECT MAX(price)
  FROM product p
  INNER JOIN c_order o
  ON p.p_code = o.p_code
  )
SELECT * FROM product WHERE price =
  (SELECT * FROM max_price
  );
```

The output will be the same as that of Listing

```
P_CODE P_NAME        PRICE LAUNCH_DT
------ ----------    ------ ---------
5      Super_Nut     30.00 30-MAR-13
6      Newer_Nut     30.00 01-MAY-13
```

You can see that our main query is cleaner, the subquery factoring helps its clarity.

The factored subquery in Listing 6.10 has more benefits as it is used more than once (i.e. twice) in the main query. The factored subquery output is the maximum price by month.

Listing 6.10: Factoring subquery

```
WITH max_price AS
  (SELECT MAX(price) max_price, extract(MONTH FROM p.launch_dt)
      launch_mth
  FROM product p
  GROUP BY extract(MONTH FROM p.launch dt)
  )
SELECT DISTINCT
  (SELECT max_price FROM max_price WHERE launch_mth < 5
  ) "Before May",
  (SELECT max_price FROM max_price WHERE launch_mth >= 5
  ) "May or After"
FROM product;
```

Running the query against the following **product** table

```
P_CODE P_NAME        PRICE LAUNCH_DT
------ ----------    ------ ---------
1      Nail          10.00 31-MAR-13
2      Washer        15.00 29-MAR-13
3      Nut           15.00 29-MAR-13
4      Screw         25.00 30-MAR-13
5      Super_Nut     20.00 30-MAR-13
6      Newer_Nut     30.00 01-MAY-13
```

Here is the factored subquery output.

```
MAX_PRICE LAUNCH_MTH
--------- ----------
       20          5
       30          3
```

And the output of the query in Listing 6.10 is this.

```
Before May  May or After
----------- ----------
30          50
```

Summary

In this chapter you learned the various types of subqueries, such as nested and correlated subqueries. In the next chapters you will apply the lesson you learned in this chapter to combine the results of two or more queries.

Chapter 7
Compound Queries

You can combine the results of two or more SELECT statements using the UNION ALL, UNION, INTERSECT, or MINUS operators. The number of output columns from every statement must be the same and the corresponding columns must have identical or compatible data types.

This chapter shows you how to combine query results.

UNION ALL

When you combine two or more queries with the UNION ALL operator, the overall output will be the total rows from all the queries. For example, take a look at the query in Listing 7.1. This query consists of two SELECT statements.

Listing 7.1: Using UNION ALL

```
SELECT p_code, p_name, 'FIRST QUERY' query
FROM product p WHERE p_name LIKE '%Nut%'
UNION ALL
SELECT p.p_code,
  p_name,
  'SECOND_QUERY' query
FROM c_order o
INNER JOIN product p
ON o.p_code = p.p_code;
```

Note that the 'FIRST QUERY' and 'SECOND_QUERY' literals in the first and second SELECT statements, respectively, are just labels to identify where a row is coming from.

Assuming that the **product** table has the following rows

P_CODE	P_NAME	PRICE	LAUNCH_DT
1	Nail	10	31-MAR-13
2	Washer	15	29-MAR-13
3	Nut	15	29-MAR-13
4	Screw	25	30-MAR-13
5	Super_Nut	30	30-MAR-13
6	New Nut	30	01-MAY-13

and the **c_order** table contains the following records

```
C_NO P_CODE  QTY ORDER_DT
---- ------ ---- ---------
10   1       100 01-APR-13
10   2       100 01-APR-13
20   1       200 01-APR-13
40   4       400 02-APR-13
40   5       400 03-APR-13
30   3       300 02-APR-13
```

the query in Listing 7.1 will return the following output.

```
P_CODE P_NAME     QUERY
------ ---------- ------------
3      Nut        FIRST QUERY
5      Super_Nut  FIRST QUERY
6      New Nut    FIRST QUERY
1      Nail       SECOND_QUERY
1      Nail       SECOND_QUERY
2      Washer     SECOND_QUERY
3      Nut        SECOND_QUERY
4      Screw      SECOND_QUERY
5      Super_Nut  SECOND_QUERY
```

Note that the output of the query in Listing 7.1 comprises all the records from the first SELECT statement followed by the rows from the second SELECT statement. You can of course use the ORDER BY clause to re-order the results. For instance, the query in Listing 7.2 modifies the query in Listing 7.1 by ordering the results on the **p_code** column using the ORDER BY clause.

Listing 7.2: Ordering output rows of a compound query

```
SELECT p_code, p_name, 'FIRST QUERY' query
FROM product p WHERE p_name LIKE '%Nut%'
UNION ALL
SELECT p.p_code,
   p_name,
   'SECOND_QUERY' query
FROM c_order o
INNER JOIN product p
ON o.p_code = p.p_code
ORDER BY p_code;
```

The result of the query in Listing 7.2 is as follows.

```
P_CODE P_NAME     QUERY
------ ---------- ------------
1      Nail       SECOND_QUERY
1      Nail       SECOND_QUERY
2      Washer     SECOND_QUERY
3      Nut        SECOND_QUERY
3      Nut        FIRST QUERY
4      Screw      SECOND_QUERY
```

```
5       Super_Nut   SECOND_QUERY
5       Super_Nut   FIRST_QUERY
6       New Nut     FIRST_QUERY
```

UNION

UNION is similar to UNION ALL. However, with UNION duplicate rows will be returned only once. As an example, consider the query in Listing 7.3 that consists of two SELECT elements.

Listing 7.3: Using UNION

```
SELECT p_code,
  p_name
FROM product p
WHERE p_name LIKE '%Nut%'
UNION
SELECT p.p_code,
  p_name
FROM c_order o
INNER JOIN product p
ON o.p_code = p.p_code
ORDER BY p_code;
```

Here is the output of the query.

```
P_CODE P_NAME
------ ---------
1       Nail
2       Washer
3       Nut
4       Screw
5       Super_Nut
6       New Nut
```

INTERSECT

When you combine two or more queries with the INTERSECT operator, the output will consist of rows common to all the participating SELECT statements. In other words, only if a row is returned by all the SELECT statements will the row be included in the final result.

Let's take a look at the example in Listing 7.4.

Listing 7.4: Using INTERSECT

```
SELECT p_code,
  p_name
FROM product p
WHERE p_name LIKE '%Nut%'
INTERSECT
```

```
SELECT p.p_code,
  p_name
FROM c_order o
INNER JOIN product p
ON o.p_code = p.p_code
ORDER BY p_code;
```

Running the query against the same **product** and **c_order** tables will return the following result.

```
P_CODE P_NAME
------ ---------
3      Nut
5      Super_Nut
```

MINUS

When you combine two SELECT statements using the MINUS operator, the final output will be rows from the first query that are not returned by the second query. Take a look at the example in Listing 7.5.

Listing 7.5: Using MINUS

```
SELECT p_code,
  p_name
FROM product p
WHERE p_name LIKE '%Nut%'
MINUS
SELECT p.p_code,
  p_name
FROM c_order o
INNER JOIN product p
ON o.p_code = p.p_code
ORDER BY p_code;
```

Running this query against the same **product** and **c_order** tables yields the following output.

```
P_CODE P_NAME
------ ---------
6      New Nut
```

With MINUS, the order of constituting SELECT statements is important. If you swap the two SELECT statements in the query in Listing 7.5, the output will be totally different. Take a look at the query in Listing 7.6, which is identical to that in Listing 7.5 except for the fact that the two SELECT statements have been swapped.

Listing 7.6: Swapping the participating SELECT statements in a query combined with MINUS

```
SELECT p.p_code,
  p_name
FROM c_order o
```

```
INNER JOIN product p
ON o.p_code = p.p_code
MINUS
SELECT p_code,
   p_name
FROM product p
WHERE p_name LIKE '%Nut%'
ORDER BY p_code;
```

The output of the query in Listing 7.6 is this:

```
P_CODE P_NAME
------ ------
1      Nail
2      Washer
4      Screw
```

Summary

In this chapter you learned that you can combine the output of two or more SELECT statements. There are five operators you can use for this purpose, UNION ALL, UNION, INTERSECT, and MINUS.

Chapter 8
Views

A view is effectively a predefined query. You create and use views most frequently for the following purposes:

- Hiding table columns (for security protection)
- Presenting pre-computed columns (in lieu of table columns)
- Hiding queries (so that the query outputs are available without running the queries)

This chapter discusses view and presents examples of views.

Creating and Using Views

You create a view using the CREATE VIEW statement. Here is its syntax.

```
CREATE VIEW view_name (columns) AS SELECT ... ;
```

The SELECT statement at the end of the CREATE VIEW statement is a predefined query. When you use a view, its predefined query is executed. Since a query result is a table that is not persisted (stored) in the database, a view is also known as a virtual table. The table in the SELECT statement of a view is known as a base table.

One of the reasons you use a view is when you have a table you need to share with other people. If you don't want some of the table columns viewable by others, you can use a view to hide those columns. You would then share the view and restrict access to the base table.

For example, Listing 8.1 shows an SQL statement for creating a view called **product_v** that is based on the **product** table. The view hides the **price** column of the base table.

Listing 8.1: Using a view to hide columns

```
CREATE VIEW product_v
  (p_code , p_name
  ) AS
SELECT p_code, p_name FROM product;
```

The **product_v** view can now be used just as you would any database table. For example, the following statement displays all columns in the **product_v** view.

```
SELECT * FROM product_v WHERE p_name NOT LIKE '%Nut%';
```

Assuming the **product** table contains these rows

```
P_CODE P_NAME      PRICE LAUNCH_DT
------ ----------- ----- ---------
1      Nail        10.00 31-MAR-13
2      Washer      15.00 29-MAR-13
3      Nut         15.00 29-MAR-13
4      Screw       25.00 30-MAR-13
5      Super_Nut   30.00 30-MAR-13
6      New Nut     30.00 01-MAY-13
```

selecting all columns from the **product_v** view will return these rows.

```
P_CODE P_NAME
------ ------
1      Nail
2      Washer
4      Screw
```

Note that within a database a view name must be unique among all the views and tables in the database.

Another use of the view is to derive computed columns not available in the base table(s). Here is an example.

Suppose the **product** table stores profit margins for each product as follows.

```
P_CODE P_NAME      PRICE LAUNCH_DT  MARGIN
------ ----------- ----- ---------  ------
1      Nail        10.00 31-MAR-13       1
2      Washer      15.00 29-MAR-13       2
3      Nut         15.00 29-MAR-13       2
4      Screw       25.00 30-MAR-13       5
5      Super_Nut   30.00 30-MAR-13       5
6      New Nut     30.00 01-MAY-13       5
```

If you want other users to see the selling price (price + margin) but not the supplier's price (price) or the margins in the **product** table, you can create a view that computes the selling price from the product price and margin, as demonstrated by the query in Listing 8.2. This query creates a view called **product_sell_v** that includes a computed column **sell_price**. The value for **sell_price** comes from the **price** and **margin** columns in the **product** table.

Listing 8.2: A view with a computed column

```
CREATE VIEW product_sell_v
  (p_no , p_name, sell_price
  ) AS
SELECT p_code, p_name, (price + margin) FROM product;
```

Selecting all data from **product_sell_v** (using "SELECT * FROM product_sell_v") returns these rows.

```
P_NO   P_NAME      SELL_PRICE
------ ----------- ----------
1      Nail                11
```

```
2        Washer              17
3        Nut                 17
4        Screw               30
5        Super_Nut           35
6        New Nut             35
```

Users of a view do not need to know the details of its predefined query. They only need to know what data is available from the view. Referring back to the self-join example in Chapter 5, "Joins", you can create the view defined in Listing 8.3 to hide the self-join query. While the rows from the **product** table only have the product code of the substitutes, this view will give you the names of their substitutes as well.

Listing 8.3: Hiding Query

```
CREATE VIEW prod_subs_v AS
SELECT prod.p_code,
  prod.p_name,
  subst.p_code subst_p_code,
  subst.p_name subst_name
FROM product prod
LEFT OUTER JOIN product subst
ON prod.s_code = subst.p_code
ORDER BY prod.p_code;
```

Recall that the **product** table has the following rows.

```
P_CODE P_NAME      PRICE LAUNCH_DT MARGIN S_CODE
------ ----------- ------ --------- ------ ------
1      Nail        10.00 31-MAR-13      1 6
2      Washer      15.00 29-MAR-13      2 7
3      Nut         15.00 29-MAR-13      2 5
4      Screw       25.00 30-MAR-13      5 NULL
5      Super_Nut   30.00 30-MAR-13      5 NULL
6      New Nut     30.00 01-MAY-13      5 NULL
```

Executing the following query that uses the view created with the statement in Listing 8.3,

```
SELECT * FROM prod_subs_v;
```

produces the following rows.

```
P_CODE P_NAME      SUBST_ SUBST_NAME
------ ----------- ------ ----------
1      Nail        6      New Nut
2      Washer      NULL   NULL
3      Nut         5      Super_Nut
4      Screw       NULL   NULL
5      Super_Nut   NULL   NULL
6      New Nut     NULL   NULL
```

Nested Views

A view can be based on another view. Such a view is called a nested view.

As an example, the **ps_noname_v** view in Listing 8.4 hides the **p_name** column and is based on the **product_sell_v** view created earlier.

Listing 8.4: A nested view
```
CREATE VIEW ps_noname_v
  (p_no , sell_price
  ) AS
SELECT p_no, sell_price FROM product_sell_v;
```

Running this statement

```
SELECT * FROM ps_noname_v;
```

will give you the following output rows

```
P_NO   SELL_PRICE
------ ----------
1              11
2              17
3              17
4              30
5              35
6              35
```

Managing Views

You can easily manage your views in Oracle. To see all views in the current database, execute the following statement.

```
SELECT VIEW_NAME FROM USER_VIEWS;
```

This will return the following output, which may differ for other databases.

```
VIEW_NAME
--------------
PRODUCT_SELL_V
PRODUCT_V
PROD_SUBS_V
PS_NONAME_V
```

To delete a view, use the DROP VIEW statement. The syntax for the DROP VIEW statement is as follows.

```
DROP VIEW view_name;
```

For example, the statement in Listing 8.5 will delete the **ps_noname_v** view.

Listing 8.5: Deleting the ps_noname_v view

```
DROP VIEW ps_nomane_v;
```

After running the statement in Listing 8.5, listing the views in the database again will give you these results.

```
VIEW_NAME
--------------
PRODUCT_SELL_V
PRODUCT_V
PROD_SUBS_V
```

Summary

A view is a predefined query that you can use to hide columns, include pre-computed columns, and so on. In this chapter you learned how to create and manage views.

Chapter 9
Built-in Functions

The Oracle database provides functions that you can use in your queries. These built-in functions can be grouped into numeric functions, character functions, datetime functions, and functions for handling null values. The objective of this chapter is to introduce you to some of these functions.

Numeric Functions

The following are some of the more important numeric functions.

ABSABS(n) returns the absolute value of n. For example, the following query returns the absolute value of (price - 20.00) as the third column.

```
SELECT p_code, price, (price - 20), ABS(price - 20.00) FROM product;
```

Applying the query to this **product** table

```
P_CODE P_NAME        PRICE LAUNCH_DT
------ ---------- ---------- ---------
1      Nail             10 31-MAR-13
2      Washer           15 29-MAR-13
3      Nut              15 29-MAR-13
4      Screw            25 30-MAR-13
5      Super_Nut        30 30-MAR-13
6      Newer_Nut        15 01-MAY-13
```

you will get this result.

```
P_CODE PRICE PRICE-20.00 ABS(PRICE-20.00)
------ ----- ----------- ----------------
1      10          -10               10
2      15           -5                5
3      15           -5                5
4      25            5                5
5      30           10               10
6      15           -5                5
```

ROUNDROUND(*n, d*) returns a number rounded to a certain number of decimal places. The argument *n* is the number to be rounded and *d* the number of decimal places. For example, the following query uses ROUND to round price to one decimal place.

```
SELECT p_code, price, ROUND (price, 1) FROM product;
```

Assuming the **product** table contains these rows

```
P_CODE P_NAME          PRICE LAUNCH_DT S_CODE
------ ---------- ---------- --------- ------
1      Nail            10.15 31-MAR-13 NULL
2      Washer          15.99 29-MAR-13 NULL
3      Nut              15.5 29-MAR-13 6
4      Screw           25.25 30-MAR-13 NULL
5      Super_Nut       30.33 30-MAR-13 NULL
6      Newer Nut       15.55 01-MAY-13 NULL
```

the output of the query is this.

```
P_CODE        PRICE ROUND(PRICE,1)
------ ---------- ---------------
1             10.15           10.2
2             15.99             16
3              15.5           15.5
4             25.25           25.3
5             30.33           30.3
6             15.55           15.6
```

SIGNSIGN(*n*) returns a value indicating the sign of n. This function returns -1 for *n* < 0, 0 for *n* = 0, and 1 for *n* > 0. As an example, the following query uses SIGN to return the sign of (price – 15).

```
SELECT p_code, price, SIGN(price - 15) FROM product;
```

Assuming the **product** table has the following records

```
P_CODE P_NAME         PRICE LAUNCH_DT
------ ---------- ------ ---------
1      Nail       10.00 31-MAR-13
2      Washer     15.00 29-MAR-13
3      Nut        15.00 29-MAR-13
4      Screw      25.00 30-MAR-13
5      Super_Nut  30.00 30-MAR-13
6      Newer Nut  15.00 01-MAY-13
```

the query output will be as follows.

```
P_CODE  PRICE SIGN(PRICE-15)
------ ------ ---------------
1      10.00             -1
2      15.00              0
3      15.00              0
4      25.00              1
5      30.00              1
```

```
6        15.00                    0
```

TRUNCTRUNC(*n, d*) returns a number truncated to a certain number of decimal places. The argument *n* is the number to truncate and *d* the number of decimal places. For example, the following query truncates **price** to one decimal place.

```
SELECT p_code, price, TRUNC(price, 1) FROM product;
```

Assuming the **product** table contains these rows

```
P_CODE P_NAME         PRICE LAUNCH_DT S_CODE
------ ---------- ---------- --------- ------
1      Nail           10.15 31-MAR-13 NULL
2      Washer         15.99 29-MAR-13 NULL
3      Nut             15.5 29-MAR-13 6
4      Screw          25.25 30-MAR-13 NULL
5      Super_Nut      30.33 30-MAR-13 NULL
6      Newer_Nut      15.55 01-MAY-13 NULL
```

the query result will be as follows.

```
P_CODE  PRICE TRUNC(PRICE,1)
------ ------ --------------
1       10.15          10.1
2       15.99          15.9
3       15.50          15.5
4       25.25          25.2
5       30.33          30.3
6       15.55          15.5
```

Character Functions

The following are some of the more important character functions.

CONCAT CONCAT(*string1, string2*) concatenates *string1* and *string2* and returns the result. If you pass a number as an argument, the number will first be converted to a string. In the following example three strings, *p_name*, a dash, and *description*, are concatenated.

```
SELECT p_code, CONCAT(CONCAT(p_name, ' -- ') , price) FROM product;
```

The **price** column value will be converted automatically to a string.

With the **product** table containing these rows

```
P_CODE P_NAME         PRICE LAUNCH_DT S_CODE
------ ---------- ---------- --------- ------
1      Nail           10.15 31-MAR-13 NULL
2      Washer         15.99 29-MAR-13 NULL
3      Nut             15.5 29-MAR-13 6
4      Screw          25.25 30-MAR-13 NULL
5      Super_Nut      30.33 30-MAR-13 NULL
6      Newer_Nut      15.55 01-MAY-13 NULL
```

executing the query against the **product** table will return this result.

```
P_CODE CONCAT(CONCAT(P_NAME,'--'),PRICE)
------ ---------------------------------
1      Nail -- 10.15
2      Washer -- 15.99
3      Nut -- 15.5
4      Screw -- 25.25
5      Super_Nut -- 30.33
6      Newer_Nut -- 15.55
```

You can also use the || operator to concatenate strings. The following query produces the same output as the one above.

```
SELECT p_code, p_name || ' -- ' || price FROM product;
```

LOWER and UPPERLOWER(*str*) converts *str* to lowercase and UPPER(*str*) converts *str* to uppercase. For example, the following query uses LOWER and UPPER.

```
SELECT p_name, LOWER(p_name), UPPER(p_name) FROM product;
```

Executing the query against the **product** table gives you this result.

```
P_NAME      LOWER(P_NAME)   UPPER(P_NAME)
----------- --------------- -------------
Nail        nail            NAIL
Washer      washer          WASHER
Nut         nut             NUT
Screw       screw           SCREW
Super_Nut   super_nut       SUPER_NUT
Newer_Nut   newer_nut       NEWER_NUT
```

LENGTHLENGTH(*str*) returns the length of string *str*. The length of a string is the number of characters in it. For example, the following query returns the length of **p_name** as the second column.

```
SELECT p_name, LENGTH(p_name) FROM product;
```

The result would look like this.

```
P_NAME      LENGTH(P_NAME)
----------- --------------
Nail                     4
Washer                   6
Nut                      3
Screw                    5
Super_Nut                9
Newer_Nut                9
```

SUBSTRSUBSTR(*str*, *start_position*, [*length*]) returns a substring of *str* starting from the position indicated by *start_position*. If *length* is not specified, the function returns a substring from *start_position* to the last character in *str*. If *length* is present, the function returns a substring which is *length* characters long starting from *start_position*. If *length* is less than 1, the function returns an empty string.

Suppose you have a **customer** table with the following rows.

```
C_NO C_NAME         PHONE
---- -------------- ---------------
10   Standard Store 1-416-223-4455
20   Quality Store  1-647-333-5566
30   Branch Office  1-416-111-2222
40   Super Agent    1-226-777-8888
```

The following query

```
SELECT SUBSTR(phone, 3) FROM customer;
```

will return the following result

```
SUBSTR(PHONE,3)
---------------
416-223-4455
647-333-5566
416-111-2222
226-777-8888
```

And the following query

```
SELECT CONCAT( SUBSTR(phone, 7, 3) , SUBSTR(phone, 11, 3)) phone
FROM customer;
```

will return this result.

```
PHONE
-------
416-223
647-333
416-111
226-777
```

Datetime Functions

The following are some of the more important datetime functions.

CURRENT_DATECURRENT DATE() returns the current date (the current date of the Oracle server at the time you run the query). For instance, the following query

```
SELECT p_code, launch_dt, CURRENT_DATE FROM product;
```

will return a result that looks like this. The actual value of the third column will depend on when you run the query.

```
P_NO LAUNCH_DT CURRENT_DATE
---- --------- ------------
1    31-MAR-13 29-APR-13
2    29-MAR-13 29-APR-13
3    29-MAR-13 29-APR-13
4    30-MAR-13 29-APR-13
```

```
5    30-MAR-13 29-APR-13
6    01-MAY-13 29-APR-13
```

TO_CHARTO_CHAR(*dt*, *fmt_specifier*) converts a date (*dt*) to a string in the format specified by *fmt_specifier*. In the following example, the **launch_dt** column is formatted with a format specifier that has three components:

- DD - the day of the month
- MONTH - the long name of the month in uppercase
- YYYY - the year

```
SELECT p_code, TO_CHAR(launch_dt, 'DD MONTH YYYY') reformatted_dt
FROM product;
```

Running the query will give you something like this.

```
P_CODE REFORMATTED_DT
------ ------------------
1      31 MARCH    2013
2      29 MARCH    2013
3      29 MARCH    2013
4      30 MARCH    2013
5      30 MARCH    2013
6      01 MAY      2013
```

NULL-related functions

The following are some of the functions that can be used to handle null values.

COALESCECOALESCE(*expr-1*, *expr-2*, ..., *expr-n*) returns the first expression from the list that is not NULL. For example, suppose your **product** table contains the following rows

```
P_CODE P_NAME     PRICE LAUNCH_DT MIN_PRICE
------ ---------- ------ --------- ---------
1      Nail       10.00 31-MAR-13 NULL
2      Washer     15.00 29-MAR-13 NULL
3      Nut        15.00 29-MAR-13     12.00
4      Screw      20.00 30-MAR-13     17.00
5      New Nut    NULL  01-APR-13     10.00
6      Newer Nut  NULL  01-MAY-13 NULL
```

and you want to view the **sale_price** column of the products using this formula:

- If price is available (not NULL) then discount it by 10%
- If price is not available then return min_price
- If both price and min_price are not available, return 5.0

You can use COALESCE to produce the correct sale_price values:

```
SELECT p_name, price, min_price,
COALESCE((price * 0.9), min_price, 5.0) sale_price
FROM product;
```

Here is the query result.

```
P_NAME       PRICE MIN_PRICE SALE_PRICE
---------    ------ --------- ----------
Nail         10.00 NULL              9
Washer       15.00 NULL           13.5
Nut          15.00     12.00      13.5
Screw        20.00     17.00        18
New Nut       NULL     10.00        10
Newer Nut     NULL  NULL            5
```

NULLIFNULLIF (*expr1*, *expr2*) compares *expr1* and *expr2*. If they are equal, the function returns null. If they are not equal, the function returns *expr1*.

Suppose you store old product prices in a table named **old_price**. The following **old_price** table, for example, shows two old prices of the Nut product, the products with p_code = 3.

```
P_CODE P_NAME       PRICE LAUNCH_DT
------ ---------    ------ ---------
3      Nut          15.00 01-MAR-10
3      Newer Nut    12.00 01-APR-12
```

Just say you want to show the old products with their current price. The following query that employs the NULLIF function can solve your problem.

```
SELECT p_code,
  p_name,
  NULLIF(p.price, op.price) current_price
FROM product p
JOIN old_product op USING (p_code);
```

Applying the query against the following **product** table and the **old_price** table

```
P_CODE P_NAME       PRICE LAUNCH_DT
------ ---------    ------ ---------
1      Nail         10.00 31-MAR-13
2      Washer       15.00 29-MAR-13
3      Better Nut   10.00 01-MAY-13
4      Screw        15.00 01-MAY-13
```

returns the two old nuts as follows

```
P_CODE P_NAME       CURRENT_PRICE
------ ---------    -------------
3      Nut                    10
3      Newer Nut              10
```

NVLNVL (*expr1*, *expr2*) returns *exprs1* if *expr1* is not NULL; otherwise, it returns *expr2*.

For example, suppose you want to compare old and current prices. Applying NVL in the following query gives you the old price from the **product** table if the product has never been superseded; otherwise, if a product has been superseded, its old price will come from the **old_product** table.

```
SELECT p_code,
   p.p_name,
   p.price current_price,
   NVL(op.price,p.price) old_price
FROM product p
LEFT OUTER JOIN old_product op USING (p_code);
```

Here is the result.

```
P_CODE P_NAME    CURRENT_PRICE  OLD_PRICE
------ --------- -------------- ----------
1      Nail                10          10
2      Washer              15          15
3      Nut                 10          12
3      Nut                 10          15
4      Screw               15          15
```

The query result shows that the only product that has been superseded is Nut, and it has been superseded twice. Therefore, its old prices are shown from the **old_product** table. The other products have never been superseded so their current and old prices are the same. Their old_price is coming from the **product** table because its **op.price** column, the first parameter of the NVL function, is NULL.

Summary

You learned some of the built-in functions that you can use in the Oracle database. If you are interested in learning more about built-in functions, consult the Oracle manual, available at Oracle website.

Chapter 10
Regular Expressions

A regular expression is a sequence of characters that describes a search pattern. This chapter explains how to use regular expressions to search for data.

Searching without Regular Expressions

You have learned that you can use queries to do exact match searches. For example, to find the customer having the name "Standard Store", your query would look like that in Listing 10.1.

Listing 10.1: Searching exactly for "Standard Store"
```
SELECT * FROM customer
WHERE c_name = 'Standard Store';
```

Assuming the **customer** table has the following columns and rows

```
C_NO C_NAME        C_ADDRESS                  C_PHONE
---- ------------- -------------------------- -----------
10 Standard Store  1 University Ave M5H 3B9    416-1010-111
20 Quality Store   3030 Bunty Lane M2K 1N9    1-905-3333-303
30 Head Office     9090 Windhaam Dr M2K1N9    647-9090-909
40 Super Agent     200 University Ave M5H3B9  2-416-2000-222
50 House Rep       5 Bayview Ln M2K 2N2       1-905-5055555
```

the output of the query in Listing 10.1 would be

```
C_NO C_NAME        C_ADDRESS                  C_PHONE
---- ------------- -------------------------- -----------
10 Standard Store  1 University Ave M5H 3B9    416-1010-111
```

You have also learned that you can use LIKE to do approximate searches. For example, the code in Listing 10.2 shows an example of LIKE. The query returns all customers with the word *Store* in their names.

Listing 10.2: Using LIKE for approximate searches
```
SELECT * FROM customer
WHERE c_name LIKE '%Store%';
```

The output would be
```
C_NO C_NAME        C_ADDRESS                  C_PHONE
```

```
---- ------------- -------------------------- ----------
10 Standard Store  1 University Ave M5H 3B9   416-1010-111
20 Quality Store   3030 Bunty Lane M2K 1N9    1-905-3333-303
```

Patterns

You can search for data based on a pattern using the REGEXP_LIKE function. For the sake of this discussion, consider the following phone number pattern, which includes the country code.

i-aaa-nnnn-nnn

where *i* is the country code, *aaa* the area code, and *nnnn-nnn* the phone number.

What if you wanted to find all phone numbers with no dash in their last seven digits? The query in Listing 10.3 would do the job.

Listing 10.3: Using a regular expression
```
SELECT * FROM customer WHERE NOT REGEXP_LIKE (c_phone,'....-...$');
```

The output would be

```
C_NO C_NAME        C_ADDRESS                  C_PHONE
---- ------------- -------------------------- ----------
50 House Rep       5 Bayview Ln M2K 2N2       1-905-5055555
```

The query in Listing 10.3 uses the REGEXP_LIKE function that has the following syntax.

```
REGEXP_LIKE(searched_string,'pattern');
```

A pattern used with REGEXP_LIKE can contain both metacharacters and ordinary characters. The pattern '....-...' in Listing 10.3, for instance, consists of the . and $ characters, which are metacharacters, and the – character, which is not a metacharacter. The $ character indicates the end of a searched string.

The pattern is searched anywhere in the searched string. In other words, it has the same effect as a LIKE clause with a surrounding pair of %. Listing 10.4 shows a rewrite of the statement in Listing 10.2. The statement in Listing 10.4 returns the same output as the statement in Listing 10.2.

Listing 10.4: Using REGEXP_LIKE in place of LIKE
```
SELECT * FROM customer WHERE REGEXP_LIKE(c_name,'Store');
```

Using Metacharacters

This section discusses metacharacters that you can use in regular expressions.

The . Metacharacter

The . character represents any one character. Listing 10.5 shows an example that uses this metacharacter.

Listing 10.5: Using the . metacharacter

```
SELECT * FROM customer WHERE NOT
REGEXP_LIKE(c_phone,'.-...-....-...');
```

Note that the dashes in the statement in Listing 10.5 are normal characters.

   Here is the output of the query.

```
C_NO C_NAME          C_ADDRESS                  C_PHONE
---- -------------    -------------------------  -----------
10 Standard Store  1 University Ave M5H 3B9   416-1010-111
30 Head Office     9090 Windhaam Dr M2K1N9   647-9090-909
50 House Rep       5 Bayview Ln M2K 2N2      1-905-5055555
```

Note that you cannot use the . metacharacter to search for NULL.

The | Metacharacter

The | metacharacter is effectively an OR operator. Listing 10.6 uses the | operator to find phone numbers having a country code 1 *or* 2.

Listing 10.6: the | operator

```
SELECT * FROM customer WHERE regexp_like(c_phone, 1|2);
```

The output would look like this.

```
C_NO C_NAME          C_ADDRESS                  C_PHONE
---- -------------    -------------------------  -----------
20 Quality Store   3030 Bunty Lane M2K 1N9    1-905-3333-303
40 Super Agent     200 University Ave M5H3B9  2-416-2000-222
50 House Rep       5 Bayview Ln M2K 2N2       1-905-5055555
```

Quantifiers

You can use the {*m*} metacharacter to avoid repeating a metacharacter. In this case, *m* is the number of repetitions. The statement in Listing 10.7 is effectively the same as the statement in Listing 10.4. However, the statement in Listing 10.7 uses the {*m*} metacharacter instead of repeating a character.

Listing 10.7: The {*m*} metacharacter

```
SELECT * FROM customer
WHERE REGEXP_LIKE(c_phone,'.-.{3}-.{4}-.{3}');
```

You can also use the {*m*} metacharacter to indicate repetitions of a normal character. For example, the statement in Listing 10.8 uses {*m*} to repeat a normal character.

Listing 10.8: Using the {m} metacharacter on a normal character

```
SELECT * FROM customer WHERE regexp_like(c_address,'a{2}');
```

Here is the result of running the statement. There is only one result since the **aa** pattern occurs only in one record.

```
C_NO C_NAME        C_ADDRESS                  C_PHONE
---- ------------- -------------------------- -----------
  30 Head Office    9090 Windhaam Dr M2K1N9    647-9090-909
```

Listing 10.9 presents another example.

Listing 10.9: The {m} on multi characters

```
SELECT * FROM customer WHERE regexp_like(c_address,'aa{3}');
```

As no customer has an address that contains three consecutive a's (*aaa*), Listing 10.9 produces no output.

The $\{m\}$ quantifier has two variants. $\{m,\}$ and $\{m, n\}$. $\{m,\}$ means *m* or more and $\{m, n\}$ means *m* or more repetitions but not greater than *n*.

There are three additional quantifiers:

- + (the plus sign) to indicate one or more characters
- ? (the question mark) to indicate zero or one occurrence of a character.
- * (the asterisk) to indicate zero or more occurrence of a character.

Listing 10.10 presents an example of a regular expression query that uses the + quantifier. It searches for any address that has an **i** followed by one or more **v**.

Listing 10.10: Using the + quantifier

```
SELECT * FROM customer WHERE regexp_like(c_address,'iv+');
```

Two addresses would be returned:

```
C_NO C_NAME        C_ADDRESS                  C_PHONE
---- ------------- -------------------------- -----------
  10 Standard Store 1 University Ave M5H 3B9   416-1010-111
  40 Super Agent    200 University Ave M5H3B9  2-416-2000-222
```

Using ()

If you want to apply the + quantifier in Listing 10.8 to **iv** instead of just **v**, put it in parentheses as in Listing 10.9.

Listing 10.11: The ()

```
SELECT * FROM customer WHERE regexp_like(c_address,'(iv)+');
```

The output would be the same, as there are only two addresses satisfying this pattern:

```
C_NO C_NAME        C_ADDRESS                  C_PHONE
---- ------------- -------------------------- -----------
  10 Standard Store 1 University Ave M5H 3B9   416-1010-111
  40 Super Agent    200 University Ave M5H3B9  2-416-2000-222
```

Using [...]

Canadian addresses use postal codes with the following pattern:

ANA NAN

where *A* is an uppercase letter and *N* a number. You can use the pattern, [A-Z][1-9][A-Z][1-9][A-Z][1-9], as shown in Listing 10.12, to search for Canadian postal codes.

Listing 10.12: Searching for Canadian postcodes

```
SELECT * FROM customer
WHERE regexp_like(c_address,'[A-Z][1-9][A-Z] [1-9][A-Z][1-9]');
```

The output would look like this:

```
C_NO C_NAME          C_ADDRESS                    C_PHONE
---- -------------- -------------------------- -----------
10 Standard Store  1 University Ave M5H 3B9    416-1010-111
20 Quality Store   3030 Bunty Lane M2K 1N9    1-905-3333-303
50 House Rep        5 Bayview Ln M2K 2N2       1-905-5055555
```

The other two rows do not qualify as their postal codes do not contain a space.

Summary

In this chapter you learned to use regular expressions to search for data.

Chapter 11
PL/SQL

PL/SQLPL/SQL, short for Procedural Language extension to SQL, complements SQL with a procedural programming language. PL/SQL is a feature of the Oracle database.

The objective of this chapter is to introduce some of the most commonly used PL/SQL features such as

- row-by-row processing of query output
- if-then-else decision logic
- exception handling
- user-defined functions

Row-by-Row Processing

You have learned in the previous chapters that a query may return multiple rows. You can write a PL/SQL program to process query output row-by-row sequentially.

The structure of the PL/SQL program for row-by-row processing is as follows.

```
BEGIN
  FOR output_row_variable IN (
    SELECT ...)
  LOOP
    row processing statements;
  END LOOP;
END;
```

For example, the program in Listing 11.1 makes use of a join query and stores its output rows in a variable named *invc*. In the processing loop, every row from *invc* is inserted into an **invoice** table.

Listing 11.1: Row-by-row processing

```
BEGIN
  FOR invc IN
  (SELECT c.c_no,
    c_name,
    p_name,
    qty,
    price unit_prc,
    (qty * price) total_prc,
```

```
      sysdate invoice_dt,
      launch_dt
   FROM c_order co
   JOIN product p  on co.p_code=p.p_code
   JOIN customer c on co.c_no=c.c_no
   )
   LOOP
       INSERT
       INTO invoice VALUES
          (
             invc.c_no,
             invc.c_name,
             invc.p_name,
             invc.qty,
             invc.unit_prc,
             invc.total_prc,
             invc.invoice_dt
          );
       END LOOP;
END;
```

Suppose you have **c_order**, **customer**, and **product** tables like the ones shown in Tables 11.1, 11.2, and 11.3, respectively, and suppose you also have an **invoice** table that is empty.

C_NO	P_CO	QTY	ORDER_DT
10	1	100	01-APR-13
10	2	100	01-APR-13
20	1	200	01-APR-13
40	4	400	02-APR-13
40	5	400	03-APR-13

Table 11.1: The c_order table

C_NO	C_NAME	C	C_DATE
10	Standard Store	1	25-JUL-13
20	Quality Store	2	27-JUL-13
30	Head Office	3	19-JUL-13
40	Super Agent	4	14-JUL-13

Table 11.2: The customer table

P_CODE	P_NAME	PRICE	LAUNCH_DT
1	Nail	10.00	31-MAR-13
2	Washer	15.00	29-MAR-13
3	Nut	15.00	29-MAR-13
4	Screw	25.00	30-MAR-13
5	Super_Nut	30.00	30-MAR-13
6	New Nut	NULL	NULL

Table 11.3: The product table

You can use the statements in Listings 11.2 to 11.6 to create and populate the tables.

Listing 11.2: Creating customer table

```
CREATE TABLE customer
  ( c_no VARCHAR(6) NOT NULL,
    c_name VARCHAR(15),
    PRIMARY KEY (c_no) );
```

Listin1g 11.3: Adding customers

```
INSERT INTO customer VALUES ( 10, 'Standard Store' );
INSERT INTO customer VALUES ( 20, 'Quality Store' );
INSERT INTO customer VALUES ( 30, 'Head Office' );
INSERT INTO customer VALUES ( 40, 'Super Agent' );
```

Listing 11.4: Creating c_order table

```
CREATE TABLE c_order
  ( c_no VARCHAR(6),
    p_code VARCHAR(6),
    qty INTEGER,
    order_dt DATE,
    FOREIGN KEY (c_no) REFERENCES customer(c_no),
    FOREIGN KEY (p_code) REFERENCES product(p_code))
;
```

Listing 11.5: Adding orders

```
INSERT INTO c_order VALUES(10,1,100, '2013-4-1');
INSERT INTO c_order VALUES(10,2,100, '2013-4-1');
INSERT INTO c_order VALUES(20,1,200, '2013-4-1');
INSERT INTO c_order VALUES(30,3,300, '2013-4-2');
INSERT INTO c_order VALUES(40,4,400, '2013-4-2');
INSERT INTO c_order VALUES(40,5,400, '2013-4-3');
```

Listing 11.6: Creating invoice table

```
CREATE TABLE invoice (   c_no VARCHAR(6),
          c_name VARCHAR (15),
          p_name VARCHAR (15),
          qty INTEGER,
          unit_prc DECIMAL(4,2),
          total_prc DECIMAL (6,2),
          invoice_dt DATE);
```

If you enter and execute the PL/SQL program in Listing 11.1 in SQL*Plus, your SQL*Plus screen will look like that in Figure 11.1. Note that to execute a PL/SQL program you need to enter the forward slash / after the last END; statement.

```
± Oracle SQL*Plus                          _ □ ✕
File  Edit  Search  Options  Help

SQL> BEGIN
  2     FOR invc IN
  3     (SELECT c_no,
  4       c_name,
  5       p_name,
  6       qty,
  7       price unit_prc,
  8       (qty * price) total_prc,
  9       sysdate invoice_dt,
 10       launch_dt
 11     FROM c_order NATURAL
 12     JOIN product NATURAL
 13     JOIN customer
 14     )
 15     LOOP
 16         INSERT
 17         INTO invoice VALUES
 18           (
 19             invc.c_no,
 20             invc.c_name,
 21             invc.p_name,
 22             invc.qty,
 23             invc.unit_prc,
 24             invc.total_prc,
 25             invc.invoice_dt
 26           );
 27     END LOOP;
 28  END;
 29  /

PL/SQL procedure successfully completed.

SQL> |
```

Figure 11.1: Executing a PL/SQL program in SQL*Plus

After the program is has been executed, the **invoice** table will be populated with the following rows.

C_NO	C_NAME	P_NAME	QTY	UNIT_PRC	TOTAL_PRC	INVOICE_DT
10	Standard Store	Washer	100	15	1500	12-SEP-13
10	Standard Store	Nail	100	10	1000	12-SEP-13
20	Quality Store	Nail	200	10	2000	12-SEP-13
40	Super Agent	Screw	400	25	10000	12-SEP-13
40	Super Agent	Super_Nut	400	30	12000	12-SEP-13

If-Then-Else Decision Logic

You can use an if statement to branch in a program. For instance, the if-then-else decision logic in Listing 11.7 treats the output rows differently based on the product launch date.

Listing 11.7: If-then-else decision logic

```
BEGIN
  FOR invc IN
  (SELECT c_no,
    c_name,
    p_name,
    qty,
    price unit_prc,
    (qty * price) total_prc,
    sysdate invoice_dt,
    launch_dt
  FROM c_order NATURAL
  JOIN product NATURAL
  JOIN customer
  )
  LOOP
    IF invc.launch_dt IS NOT NULL THEN
      INSERT
      INTO invoice VALUES
        (
          invc.c_no,
          invc.c_name,
          invc.p_name,
          invc.qty,
          invc.unit_prc,
          invc.total_prc,
          invc.invoice_dt
        );
    ELSE
      NULL;
    END IF;
  END LOOP;
END;
```

For this example, I use a **c_order** table with the following rows.

```
C_NO P_CO  QTY ORDER_DT
---- ----  ---- ---------
10   1     100 01-APR-13
10   2     100 01-APR-13
20   1     200 01-APR-13
40   4     400 02-APR-13
40   5     400 03-APR-13
40   6     600 01-MAY-13
```

The difference between this **c_order** table and the one used in the previous example is that this table has a sixth row that records the sale of a product (p_co = 6) with a null launch_dt.

Because the product's launch_dt is NULL, the process does not insert an invoice row for this additional order. If you execute the program in Listing 11.7, the same rows as in the previous example will be inserted into the invoice table.

Exception Handling

PL/SQL allows you to handle errors (or exceptions) in your program using the EXCEPTION statement. Its syntax is as follows.

```
EXCEPTION
WHEN exception_name
THEN exception_handling_statement;
```

For example, suppose you want to query a specific invoice from an invoice table using the PL/SQL program in Listing 11.8. The SELECT INTO query in Listing 11.8 stores its output rows into an **invc** variable, which is declared to have a ROWTYPE data type.

Listing 11.8: PL/SQL program without exception handling
```
DECLARE
  invc invoice%ROWTYPE;
BEGIN
  SELECT *
  INTO invc
  FROM invoice
  WHERE c_no = '&c_no_prompt'
  AND p_name = '&p_name_prompt'
  AND TO_CHAR(invoice_dt, 'DD-MON-YY') = '&invoice_dt_prompt';
  dbms_output.put_line(invc.c_name || ' - ' || invc.p_name || ' - ' ||
      invc.total_prc);
END;
```

Assume the **invoice** table has the following rows.

C_NO	C_NAME	P_NAME	QTY	UNIT_PRC	TOTAL_PRC	INVOICE_DT
10	Standard Store	Washer	100	15	1500	12-SEP-13
10	Standard Store	Nail	100	10	1000	12-SEP-13
20	Quality Store	Nail	200	10	2000	12-SEP-13
40	Super Agent	Screw	400	25	10000	12-SEP-13
40	Super Agent	Super_Nut	400	30	12000	12-SEP-13

If you execute the program in Listing 11.8, you will be prompted three times to enter the invoice's **c_no**, **p_name**, and **invoice_dt** you are querying. If the invoice is not available in the **invoice** table, the program will abort and you will see a "no data found" error message. Your SQL*Plus should look like this.

```
SQL> DECLARE
  2     invc invoice%ROWTYPE;
  3  BEGIN
  4     SELECT *
  5     INTO invc
  6     FROM invoice
  7     WHERE c_no = '&c_no_prompt'
  8     AND p_name = '&p_name_prompt'
  9     AND TO_CHAR(invoice_dt, 'DD-MON-YY') = '&invoice_dt_prompt';
 10     dbms_output.put_line(invc.c_name || ' - ' || invc.p_name || ' - '
       || invc.total_prc);
```

```
 11  END;
 12  /
Enter value for c_no_prompt: 10
old    7:    WHERE c_no = '&c_no_prompt'
new    7:    WHERE c_no = '10'
Enter value for p_name_prompt: Nail
old    8:    AND p_name = '&p_name_prompt'
new    8:    AND p_name = 'Nail'
Enter value for invoice_dt_prompt: 11-SEP-13
old    9:    AND TO_CHAR(invoice_dt, 'DD-MON-YY') = '&invoice_dt_prompt';
new    9:    AND TO_CHAR(invoice_dt, 'DD-MON-YY') = '11-SEP-13';
DECLARE
*
ERROR at line 1:
ORA-01403: no data found
ORA-06512: at line 4


SQL>
```

To handle an error (exception), you can add an exception-handling statement to the program in Listing 11.8. Listing 11.9 shows a modified version of the program in Listing 11.8. There is an exception handler in the program in Listing 11.9.

Listing 11.9: With Exception Handling

```
DECLARE
  invc invoice%ROWTYPE;
BEGIN
  SELECT *
  INTO invc
  FROM invoice
  WHERE c_no                            = '&c_no_prompt'
  AND p_name                            = '&p_name_prompt'
  AND TO_CHAR(invoice_dt, 'DD-MON-YY') = '&invoice_dt_prompt';
  dbms_output.put_line(invc.c_name || ' - ' || invc.p_name || ' - ' ||
      invc.total_prc);
EXCEPTION
WHEN no_data_found THEN
  dbms_output.put_line('Error: The invoice does not exist!');
END;
```

If the invoice you are querying is not in the invoice table, the WHEN no_data_found will trap and handle the error, and displays its message. In other words, the program will not abort. To see the exception-handler's message, issue a **set serveroutput on** command before you execute the program. The SQL*Plus console will look like this.

```
SQL> set serveroutput on;
SQL> DECLARE
  2    invc invoice%ROWTYPE;
  3  BEGIN
  4    SELECT *
  5    INTO invc
  6    FROM invoice
```

```
  7     WHERE c_no                              = '&c_no_prompt'
  8     AND p_name                              = '&p_name_prompt'
  9     AND TO_CHAR(invoice_dt, 'DD-MON-YY') = '&invoice_dt_prompt';
 10     dbms_output.put_line(invc.c_name || ' - ' || invc.p_name || ' - '
        || invc.total_prc);
 11  EXCEPTION
 12  WHEN no_data_found THEN
 13     dbms_output.put_line('Error: The invoice does not exist!');
 14  END;
 15  /
Enter value for c_no_prompt: 10
old   7:    WHERE c_no                              = '&c_no_prompt'
new   7:    WHERE c_no                              = '10'
Enter value for p_name_prompt: Nails
old   8:    AND p_name                              = '&p_name_prompt'
new   8:    AND p_name                              = 'Nails'
Enter value for invoice_dt_prompt: 12-SEP-13
old   9:    AND TO_CHAR(invoice_dt, 'DD-MON-YY') = '&invoice_dt_prompt';
new   9:    AND TO_CHAR(invoice_dt, 'DD-MON-YY') = '12-SEP-13';
Error: The invoice does not exist!

PL/SQL procedure successfully completed.

SQL>
```

User-defined Functions

You have learned Oracle built-in functions in Chapter 9, "Built-in Functions." Using PL/SQL you can write your own functions. The syntax for a user-defined function is as follows.

```
CREATE FUNCTION FUNCTION name(parameters)
   RETURN data_type
  IS
   Variable_declarations
  BEGIN
   Processing_statements
  EXCEPTION
   Exception_handling statements
END;
```

For example, Listing 11.10 shows a user-defined function named **calc_new_price**. The function takes two parameters and uses the values of the parameters to calculate a new price and returns the result. If you execute the statement in Listing 11.10, a stored function named **calc_new_price** will be created and stored in your database.

Listing 11.10: Creating function calc_new_price

```
CREATE FUNCTION calc_new_price(
     exist_price NUMBER,
     change_percentage NUMBER)
   RETURN NUMBER
```

```
   IS
   BEGIN
     RETURN exist_price + (exist_price * change_percentage);
   END;
```

Now you can use the function just like you would any Oracle built-in function. The update statement in Listing 11.11, for example, uses the **calc_new_price** function to calculate new prices and update the product prices.

Listing 11.11: Using the calc_new_price function

```
UPDATE product SET price = calc_new_price(price, 0.1) ;
```

Stored Procedures

While a function returns a value, a procedure does some actions. Here is the syntax of the statement that creates a stored procedure.

```
CREATE PROCEDURE procedure (parameters) AS
  Variables declaration;
  BEGIN
  statements;
END procedure;
```

The stored procedure **increase_price** created by the statement in Listing 11.12 increases the prices of those products if their current prices are lower than the average price of all products.

The procedure does not have any parameter. A variable **avgprc** is declared as a number with two decimals.

If you run the code in Listing 11.12, the **increase_price** procedure will be created and stored in the database as a database object.

Listing 11.12: Stored Procedure

```
CREATE PROCEDURE increase_price
AS
  avgprc NUMBER(6,2);
BEGIN
  SELECT AVG(price) INTO avgprc FROM product;
  UPDATE product SET price = price + (price * 0.10) WHERE price < avgprc;
END increase_price;
```

You call (execute) a stored procedure in a PL/SQL program as a statement by iteself: increase_price, as shown in Listing 11.13.

Listing 11.13: Calling Procedure

```
BEGIN
Increase_price;
END;
```

Anonymous and Stored programs

Both user-defined functions (a.k.a. stored functions) and stored procedures are PL/SQL programs with names. You give them names when you create them.

PL/SQL program that is not created using a CREATE statement is called anonymous and does not have a name.

Triggers

A trigger is a named program unit that is stored in the database and fired (executed) in response to a specified event. The event can be, for example, a DELETE, INSERT, or UPDATE statement.

The syntax of the CREATE TRIGGER is as follows.

```
CREATE TRIGGER trigger
BEFORE | AFTER
DELETE | OR INSERT | OR UPDATE
ON table
PL/SQL block
```

The **t_prodlog** trigger created in Listing 11.14 is fired when a DELETE or INSERT statement is executed against the **product** table.

When the trigger is fired, the PL/SQL program (which is simply an INSERT statement in this trigger) is executed before a row with one column, the current date is added into the **prodlog** table.

Listing 11.14: Trigger
```
CREATE TRIGGER t_prodlog
  BEFORE DELETE OR INSERT ON product
BEGIN
  INSERT INTO prodlog (log_date)
    VALUES (SYSDATE);
END;
```

To test the **t_prodlog** trigger, you need to create a **prodlog** table using the statement in Listing 11.15.

Listing 11.15: Creating prodlog table
```
CREATE TABLE t_prodlog (log_date DATE, p_code VARCHAR2(6));
```

Adding Conditions to A Trigger

You can add a condition to a trigger to determine when a trigger should fire. The statement in Listing 11.16 is an example of a conditioned trigger that uses a FOR EACH ROW WHEN clause. Because of the condition, the trigger will only be fired if the new unit price is greater than 11.0.

Listing 11.16: Conditioned Trigger
```
CREATE TRIGGER t_prodlog_when AFTER
  UPDATE ON product FOR EACH ROW WHEN (NEW.price > 10.00) BEGIN
  INSERT INTO prodlog
    (log_date
    ) VALUES
    (SYSDATE
```

```
   );
END;
```

On top of the WHEN condition, you can further restrict a trigger by specifying specific columns on the UPDATE clause. The trigger in Listing 11.17 will only fire when updating the **unit_price** column.

Listing 11.17: A trigger that fires on a column update

```
CREATE TRIGGER t_prodlog_when AFTER
  UPDATE OF PRICE ON product FOR EACH ROW WHEN (NEW.price > 10.00) BEGIN
  INSERT INTO prodlog (log_date )
  VALUES (SYSDATE);
END;
```

Listing 11.18 presents an example trigger that calls the **increase_price** stored procedure that we created earlier.

Listing 11.18: Trigger calling a stored procedure

```
BEGIN
  increase_price;
END;
```

Transactions

A transaction is a a group of SQL statements. You control the grouped statements so that data changes are committed or rolled back. To commit data changes, use the COMMIT statement. To roll back changes, use the ROLLBACK statement.

The program in Listing 11.19 has two UPDATE statements that change the data in the **product** table. The first UPDATE statement starts a transaction. If after the price updates the average price is greater than 25.00, the two updates will be rolled back; otherwise they will be committed. The commit or rollback ends the transaction.

Listing 11.19: Commit and Rollback

```
CREATE PROCEDURE incprc_comrlb
AS
  avgprc NUMBER(6,2);
BEGIN
  SELECT AVG(price) INTO avgprc FROM product;
  UPDATE product SET price = price + (price * 0.10) WHERE price < avgprc;
  UPDATE product SET price = price + (price * 0.01) WHERE price > avgprc;
  SELECT AVG(price) INTO avgprc FROM product;
  IF avgprc > 25.00 THEN ROLLBACK;
  END IF;
  COMMIT;
END incprc_comrlb;
```

Savepoints

Within a transaction you can set a savepoint to set the boundary of a rollback. In Listing 11.20 we set a savepoint named **after_insert** after an INSERT statement. If a rollback occurs, the changes will roll back to right before the SAVEPOINT statement, i.e. only the insert will be rolled back, the first update will not.

Listing 11.20: Using a savepoint

```
CREATE PROCEDURE incprc_savepoint
AS
   avgprc NUMBER(6,2);
BEGIN
   SELECT AVG(price) INTO avgprc FROM product;
   UPDATE product SET price = price + (price * 0.10) WHERE price < avgprc;
   INSERT INTO product VALUES
     (999,'New Hammer',45.50,'1-5-2013'
     );
   SAVEPOINT after_insert;
   UPDATE product SET price = price + (price * 0.01) WHERE price > avgprc;
   SELECT AVG(price) INTO avgprc FROM product;
   IF avgprc > 25.00 THEN
     ROLLBACK TO after_insert;
   END IF;
   COMMIT;
END incprc_savepoint;
```

Multiple Transactions

A program can have more than one transaction. You start a transaction by issuing a SET TRANSACTION statement and terminate it with a COMMIT or ROLLBACK statement.

The SET TRANSACTION statement has the following syntax.

```
SET TRANSACTION 'transaction';
```

The program in Listing 11.21 has two transactions, **t1** and **t2**. If a rollback occurs, the changes rolled back will only be within **t2**.

Listing 11.21: Savepoint

```
CREATE PROCEDURE multitrans
AS
   avgprc NUMBER(6,2);
BEGIN
   SET TRANSACTION NAME 't1';
   INSERT INTO product VALUES
     (999,'New Hammer',45.50,to_date('1-5-2013','DD-MM-YYYY'));
     COMMIT;
   SET TRANSACTION NAME 't2';
   UPDATE product SET price = price + (price * 0.10) WHERE price > avgprc;
   SELECT AVG(price) INTO avgprc FROM product;
   IF avgprc > 25.00 THEN
     ROLLBACK;
   END IF;
   COMMIT;
END multitrans;
```

Summary

In this chapter you learned several PL/SQL features. However, what's presented here is just the tip of the iceberg. PL/SQL has many other features that you will need in real-world application development. These other features are unfortunately beyond the scope of this book.

Chapter 12
Granting Permissions

When you create a table, a view, or a PL/SQL program, you become the owner of the database object. In order for other users to view or access your database object, you must first grant them appropriate permissions using the GRANT statement.

This chapter explains how to grant permissions to a user or a group of users to access a database object.

Using the GRANT Statement

The GRANT statement has the following syntax.

```
GRANT privilege
ON object
TO user;
```

Some database objects require special privileges. The following sections show the privileges you need to grant on a table, aview, or a PL/SQL program.

Granting Permissions to Access A Table

To allow others to manipulate the data in a table, you can grant one or more of the SELECT, INSERT, UPDATE, and DELETE privileges. Listing 12.1 grants all four privileges on the **product** table to user **user1**.

Listing 12.1: Granting data manipulation privileges
```
GRANT SELECT| INSERT| UPDATE| DELETE ON product
TO user1;
```

If you want to try the program in Listing 12.1, you first need to run the query in Listing 12.2.

Listing 12.2: Creating user user1
```
CREATE USER user1
IDENTIFIED by password1;
GRANT CREATE SESSION to user1;
```

User **user1** can now manipulate the data in the **product** table. You can now log on (connect) as user1 and query the **product** table using the query in Listing 12.3.

Listing 12.3: Testing the granted privilege

```
SELECT * FROM djoni.product WHERE price = 20.00;
```

Note that **user1** needs to prefix the **product** table with the owner's username (djoni) to specifically query the **product** table owned by that user.

For UPDATE and INSERT privileges you can grant selective columns. The syntax for granting selective columns is as follows.

```
GRANT
UPDATE|INSERT(columns) ON table TO user;
```

For instance, the code in Listing 12.4 grants the update privilege on the **c_name** column of the **customer** table.

Listing 12.4: Granting selective column

```
GRANT
UPDATE(c_name) ON customer TO user1;
```

Note that you cannot grant delete and select privileges on selective columns.

Granting Permissions to Access A View

The grant on a view is the same as that on a table. For instance, the code in Listing 12.5 grants the **vx** view to **user1** for select and update.

Listing 12.5: Granting view

```
GRANT
SELECT, UPDATE ON vx TO user1;
```

Granting to Public

Instead of granting a privilege to specific users, you can grant to all users using the following statement.

```
GRANT privilege
ON object
TO PUBLIC;
```

The code in Listing 12.6 grants the select privilege on the **product** table to all users.

Listing 12.6: Granting Role

```
GRANT SELECT ON djoni.product TO PUBLIC;
```

Granting to A Role

A role is a set of privileges. It is a three steps process. First, you create a role. Then, you grant privileges to the role. Finally, you grant the role to the intended users.

Listing 12.7 illustrates the process. It first creates a role called **ins_del**, and then gives the role insert and delete privileges on the **vx** view. Finally, it grants the **ins_del** role to user **user1**.

Listing 12.7: Granting a role

```
CREATE role ins_del;
GRANT ALL ON vx TO ins_del;
GRANT ins_del TO user1;
```

Granting to A PL/SQL Program

To allow other users to execute your program, you must grant them the EXECUTE privilege. Listing 12.8 shows a statement that grants user1 the permission to execute the **calc_new_price** function created in Chapter 10.

Listing 12.8: Granting program

```
GRANT EXECUTE ON calc_new_price TO user1;
```

Summary

When you create a view, a table, or a PL/SQL program, you become the owner of the database object. This means, by default, the database object is only accessible to you. To allow other users to access your database object, you must grant them privileges to do so.

Chapter 13
The Data Dictionary

The data dictionary of a database contains data about the data in the database. This data about data is also known as metadata. The data in the data dictionary is stored as tables. As such, you can use your SQL skills to query the data dictionary of your database. The tables and their data are maintained by the Oracle database system. You should not access the dictionary tables directly. Instead, use the Oracle-supplied views of the dictionary.

This chapter explores the views in the data dictionary.

The Dictionary View

The dictionary view is one of the views in the data dictionary. It returns all the views available in your dictionary. The view has two columns and can have over 650 rows.

The query in Listing 13.1 can be used to list all the views in the data dictionary.

Listing 13.1: Exploring the data dictionary
```
SELECT * FROM dictionary;
```

Here is partial output of the query in Listing 11.1. Remember, the actual output has many more rows.

```
TABLE_NAME              COMMENTS
------------------      ------------------------------------------------
ALL_XML_SCHEMAS         Description of all XML Schemas that user has
                        privilege to reference
ALL_XML_SCHEMAS2        Dummy version of ALL_XML_SCHEMAS that does not
                        have an XMLTYPE column
USER_RESOURCE_LIMITS    Display resource limit of the user
USER_PASSWORD_LIMITS    Display password limits of the user
USER_CATALOG            Tables, Views, Synonyms and Sequences owned by
                        the user
ALL_CATALOG             All tables, views, synonyms, sequences
                        accessible to the user
USER_CLUSTERS           Descriptions of user's own clusters
ALL_CLUSTERS            Description of clusters accessible to the user
USER_CLU_COLUMNS        Mapping of table columns to cluster column~
USER_COL_COMMENTS       Comments on columns of user's tables and
```

You will learn some of the views in the next sections.

The user_catalog View

The **user_catalog** view stores the names of your tables and views. Use the query in Listing 13.2 to see the tables and views that you have in your database. These tables and views are known as user tables and views (as opposed to system tables and views).

Listing 13.2: Using the user_catalog view

```
SELECT * FROM user_catalog;
```

The query output from running the query in Listing 13.2 in your database may not be exactly the same as what I have got here. Here is mine.

```
TABLE_NAME       TABLE_TYPE
---------------  ----------
CUSTOMER         TABLE
C_ORDER          TABLE
PRODUCT          TABLE
C_SHIP           TABLE
OLD_PRODUCT      TABLE
PRICE_LOG        TABLE
PROD_SUBST       TABLE
SHIPMENT         TABLE
PRODUCT_SELL_V   VIEW
PRODUCT_V        VIEW
PROD_SUBS_V      VIEW
PS_NONAME_V      VIEW
```

The user_tab_cols View

To see the details of each table and view, you can query the **user_tab_cols** view. For example, the query in Listing 13.3 shows you the name, data type, length, precision, and scale of each column in the **product** table.

Listing 13.3: Finding out the columns metadata of the product table

```
SELECT column_name,
   data_type,
   data_length,
   data_precision,
   data_scale
FROM user_tab_cols
WHERE table_name = 'PRODUCT';
```

Here is the query output.

```
COLUMN_NAME DATA_TYPE DATA_LENGTH DATA_PRECISION DATA_SCALE
----------- --------- ----------- -------------- ----------
```

```
P_CODE       VARCHAR2          6
P_NAME       VARCHAR2         14
PRICE        NUMBER           22              4           2
LAUNCH_DT    DATE              7
```

In addition to these five columns, the **user_tab_cols** view contains many other columns, such as those for showing the owner and the default value of a table or a view.

The user_constraints View

You can query the **user_constraints** view to find out the constraints you have on a table. Listing 11.4 shows an example to query the constraints of the **new_product** table.

Listing 13.4: Constraints metadata of the new_product table
```
SELECT CONSTRAINT_NAME,
  CONSTRAINT_TYPE,
  SEARCH_CONDITION
FROM user_constraints
WHERE TABLE_NAME = 'NEW_PRODUCT';
```

Here is the query output. The C, P, U values in the **constraint_type** column stand for Check, Primary key, and Unique, respectively.

```
CONSTRAINT_NAME CONSTRAINT_TYPE   SEARCH_CONDITION
--------------- ----------------  -----------------
SYS_C0030881    C                 LAUNCH_DT IS NOT NULL
SYS_C0030882    C                 price < 100.00
SYS_C0030883    P
SYS_C0030884    U
```

The user_procedures View

The **user_procedures** view contains information about your stored programs, including functions, procedures and triggers. Use the query in Listing 11.5 to show your stored programs. Note that this view has some other columns that provide more information about the stored programs.

Listing 13.5: Revealing the metadata of stored procedures and functions
```
SELECT object_name, object_type FROM user_procedures;
```

Executing the query against your database will give you something like the following output rows.

```
OBJECT_NAME       OBJECT_TYPE
----------------  -----------
CALC_NEW_PRICE    FUNCTION
UPD_PRICE         PROCEDURE
PRICE_UPD_LOGGING TRIGGER
```

The user_source View

The **user_source** view contains the source code of your stored functions. For example, the query in Listing 11.6 returns the source of the **CALC_NEW_PRICE** function.

Listing 13.6: Reading the source code of a function

```
SELECT line, text FROM user_source WHERE name = 'CALC_NEW_PRICE';
```

Executing the query will show you the lines of codes of the function as shown here.

```
NAME              TYPE       LINE TEXT
----------------  --------   ----------------------------------------
CALC_NEW_PRICE    FUNCTION     1 FUNCTION calc_new_price(
CALC_NEW_PRICE    FUNCTION     2       exist_price NUMBER,
CALC_NEW_PRICE    FUNCTION     3       inc          NUMBER)
CALC_NEW_PRICE    FUNCTION     4    RETURN NUMBER
CALC_NEW_PRICE    FUNCTION     5    IS
CALC_NEW_PRICE    FUNCTION     6    BEGIN
CALC_NEW_PRICE    FUNCTION     7      RETURN exist_price + (exist_price *
                                      inc);
CALC_NEW_PRICE    FUNCTION     8    END;
```

Summary

The data dictionary contains the metadata of your database. In this chapter you learned to use some of the views in the data dictionary.

Appendix A
Installing Oracle Database XE

To try out the examples in this book, you need an Oracle database. Because you need to create tables and other objects, as well as store and update data, it is best if you have your own database. Fortunately, you can download Oracle Database Express Edition (a.k.a. XE) for free from Oracle's website. As you will learn in this appendix, Oracle Database XE comes with a tool called SQL*Plus that you can use to run SQL statements.

Downloading Oracle Database XE

This database software can be downloaded from this web page.

```
http://www.oracle.com/technetwork/indexes/downloads/index.html
```

Scroll down until you see Database 11g Express Edition on the list and click the link. Then, select the version for your platform (Windows or Unix) and follow the download instructions. You will be requested to accept the license agreement and, if you don't have one already, create an account. Don't worry, creating an account is free.

Note
The book examples are tested on Windows. They should work equally well on Linux. The following installation guide is for Windows only.

Installing Oracle Database XE

Unzip the downloaded file to a folder in your local drive, then double-click the setup.exe file. You will see the Install Wizard welcome window like that in Figure A.1.

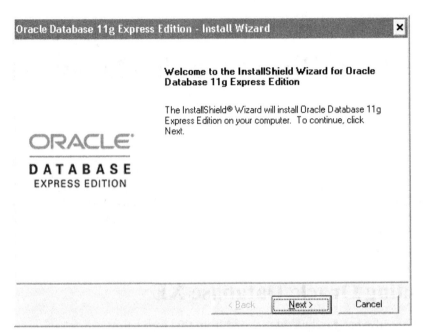

Figure A.1: The Welcome page of the Install Wizard

Click the Next button, accept the agreement on the License Agreement window, and click the Next button. The next window that will appear is the "Choose Destination Location" window like the one in Figure A.2.

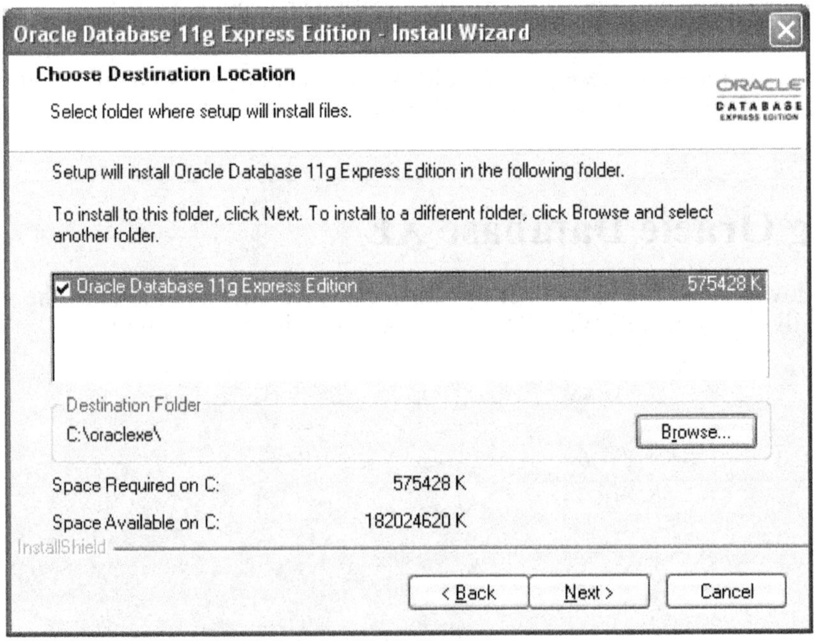

Figure A.2: Choosing the installation destination

Click the Browse button and navigate to a directory of your choice, then click the Next button. If you are prompted to enter port numbers, just accept the defaults (you might need to change, if for example the suggested default port numbers are already used). After that, click the Next button. You will be presented with the Passwords window (See Figure A.3)

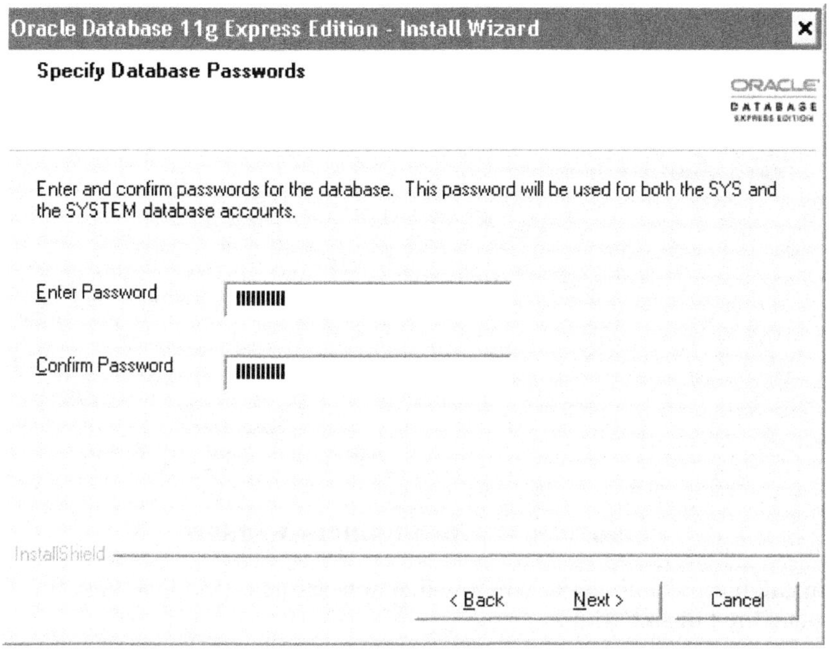

Figure A.3: Entering and confirming the password

Enter your password and confirm it. Make a note of this password as you will need it. Note that this password is for both the SYS and SYSTEM accounts. Then, click the Next button and you will see the Summary window (See Figure A.4)

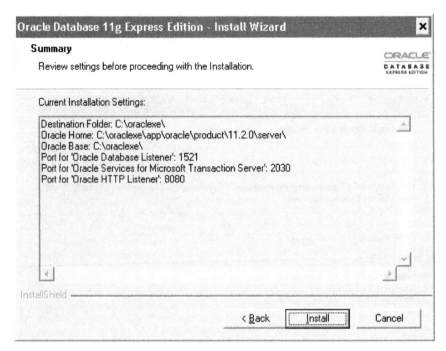

Figure A.4: The Summary window

Click the Install button, and on the window that appears next (the Installation Completion window), click the Finish button.

The next section shows you how to create a database user that you will use to test the book examples.

Creating a User with SQL*Plus

To create a database user and to run an SQL statement, use SQL*Plus. SQL*Plus is a tool that comes with the Oracle database. To run SQL*Plus, select "Run SQL…" from your Windows Start menu, as shown in Figure A.5.

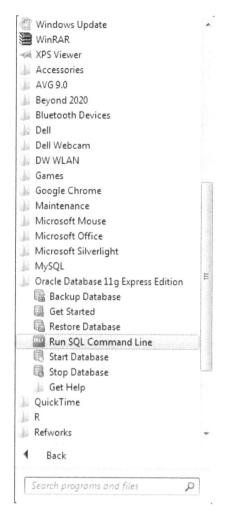

Figure A.5: Selecting the Run SQL Command Line

SQL*Plus will open, as shown in Figure A.6. SQL*Plus is the command-line console client of the Oracle database. You use it, among other things, to enter and execute SQL statements and PL/SQL programs.

Figure A.6: The SQL*Plus console

Connect as SYSTEM by typing the following command and pressing Enter

```
CONNECT SYSTEM/password AS SYSDBA;
```

Here, *password* is the password of the SYSTEM user you entered during installation. To create a user, enter and execute the following command.

```
CREATE USER name IDENTIFIED BY password;
```

Replace *name* with the actual user name you want to create and *password* with a password. For example, the following command creates a user named john with password secret.

```
CREATE USER john IDENTIFIED BY secret;
```

Next, enter and execute the following command, replacing *name* with the user name used in the previous command:

```
GRANT ALL PRIVILEGES TO name;
```

The GRANT ALL command gives the specified users all available permissions. Giving a user all privileges may not be a wise thing to do in a real life system.

The user now has permissions to test the book examples. To log on, enter this command to SQL*Plus.

```
CONNECT name/password;
```

For example

```
CONNECT john/secret;
```

A database named "XE" was created during installation. The CONNECT command above connects you to this database.

You are now set to test the book examples.

Appendix B
Oracle Built-in Data Types

The Oracle database has a total of 18 built-in data types. These data types are shown in Table B.1.

Data Type	Description
VARCHAR2(*ml*)	Variable-length character string having a maximum length of *ml*
NVARCHAR2(*ml*)	The Unicode version of VARCHAR2
NUMBER(*p*, *s*)	Number having precision *p* and scale *s*
DATE	Valid date ranging from January 1, 4712 BC, to December 31, 9999 AD
BINARY_FLOAT	32-bit floating point number
BINARY_DOUBLE	64-bit floating point number
TIMESTAMP	The year, month, and day values of the date, plus the hour, minute, and second values of the time
INTERVAL YEAR	Stores a period of time in years and months
INTERVAL DAY	Stores a period of time in days, hours, minutes, and seconds
RAW(*size*)	Raw binary data of the length of *size* bytes
LONG RAW	The larger version of RAW
ROWID	Base-64 string representing the unique address of a row in its table
CHAR(*l*)	Fixed-length character string having length *l*
NCHAR(*l*)	Unicode version of CHAR
CLOB	A character large object containing single-bytes or multi-byte characters
NCLOB	Unicode version of CLOB
BLOB	A binary large object
BFILE	Contains the locator to a large binary file stored outside the database

Table B.1: Oracle Built-in Data Types

Appendix C
Indexes

An index entry of the Index section of a book points to the location of the word/phrase indicated by the entry. The index entry helps you find the pages containing the word/phrase. Similarly, a column index of a table can speed up finding your data in a database. If your query has a condition on a column (or columns) that is (are) not indexed, the table will be fully scanned and the query will be slower than if an index was available.

This appendix shows you how to create various indexes. The topics covered are as follows.

- Creating an index
- Multi-column indexes
- Bit map and join bit map indexes
- Function-based indexes
- Deleting an index

Creating an Index

To create an index on a column or columns of a table, use this statement.

```
CREATE INDEX index ON table (columns);
```

For example, the statement in Listing C.1 creates an index named **p_name_ix** on the **p_name** column of the **product** table.

Listing C.1: Creating an index on the p_name in the product table
```
CREATE INDEX p_name_ix ON product (p_name);
```
Unique Index Names and Columns
You cannot have duplicate index names. In addition, you cannot have the same column(s) indexed more than once.

Multi-Column Indexes

An index can be based on multiple columns. A multi-column index is useful if you need to search on rows having the same value on an indexed column. For instance, if your query has to search on the **p_name** column of the **product** table and there can be more than one row with the same **p_name** but with different launch dates, it would help if you create an index on both **p_name** and **launch_dt**.

As an example, the statement in Listing C.2 creates a multi-column index on the **p_name** and **launch_dt** columns of the **product** table.

Listing C.2: Creating an index on multiple columns

```
CREATE INDEX p_name_launch_ix ON product (p_name, launch_dt);
```

Bitmap Indexes

The indexes created in Listings C.1 and C.2 are ordinary indexes, which are technically called B-tree indexes. Another type of index, the bitmap index, can be a better choice for tables whose rows will not be changed concurrently, such as in a low-volume data entry environment. A product table is an example of such low data maintenance and therefore is suitable for bitmap indexes. By contrast, a customer order table gets rows inserted more frequently and is not a good candidate for bitmap indexes.

For example, the statement in Listing C.3 creates a bitmap index named **order_bix** on the **c_order** table.

Listing C.3: Creating a bitmap index

```
CREATE BITMAP INDEX order_bix ON c_order (p_code, c_no);
```

Bitmap Join Indexes

The bitmap join index is a variant of the bitmap index. The bitmap join index is specifically created to expedite column retrieval from a joined table in a join query.

For example, the statement in Listing C.4 creates a bitmap join index on a **c_name** column. Note that the syntax for creating a bitmap join index has additional clauses, FROM and WHERE. These clauses define the join of the tables.

Listing C.4: Creating a bitmap join index on the c_name column

```
CREATE BITMAP INDEX c_name_bji ON c_order(c.c_name)
FROM c_order o, customer c
WHERE o.c_no = c.c_no;
```

c_name can now be retrieved faster using the index than if it has to be scanned from the **c_order** table.

While the aim of having a bitmap join index is to expedite a specific column retrieval (**c_name** in the statement in Listing C.4), joining tables generally makes use of the primary key indexes of the tables as they are mostly joined on these keys. If you often need to join on other columns, you may want to create indexes on these columns as well.

Function-based Indexes

There are often cases where capitalization is used inconsistently when entering data into a table. Sometimes, a column value is entered in all capitals, sometimes in lowercase, and sometimes in mixed cases.

For example, the following customer table shows inconsistent capitalization has been used for the **c_name** column.

```
C_NO  C_NAME          PHONE
----  --------------  --------------
10    Standard Store  1-416-223-4455
20    Quality store   1-647-333-5566
30    Branch Office   1-416-111-2222
40    Super Agent     1-226-777-8888
50    New Brand       1-905-777-9999
60    NEW STORE       1-905-000-9999
```

This poses a problem because a query may not return all the data intended. For example, in the case of the customer table above, searching on "new store" will not find "NEW STORE." To get around this problem, you can use the UPPER function in your query, as shown in Listing C.5.

Listing C.5: Using the UPPER function in a query

```
SELECT * FROM customer WHERE UPPER(c_name) LIKE '%STORE';
```

For this query to run faster, you should also create an index that is based on the UPPER-ed version of the **c_name** column. Listing C.6 shows how to do it.

Listing C.6: A function-based index

```
CREATE INDEX func_name_ix ON customer
  (UPPER(c_name)
  ) ;
```

Deleting An Index

To delete an index of any type, use the DROP INDEX statement. For example, the statement in Listing C.7 deletes the **s_name_bji** index.

Listing C.7: Deleting a bitmap join index

```
DROP INDEX s_name_bji;
```

Appendix D
Oracle SQL Developer

Real world database programmers usually use an Integrated Development Environment (IDE) when developing database applications. The Oracle SQL Developer is an IDE especially suitable for developing and maintaining Oracle database applications. It is available as a free download from the Oracle website.

This appendix is a guide to installing and setting up the Oracle SQL Developer. It also shows you how to use some of its features.

Downloading and Installing SQL Developer

This section provides details on how to download SQL Developer and install it on a Windows computer.

You can download SQL Developer from this Oracle website:

```
http://www.oracle.com/technetwork/indexes/downloads/
```

Scroll down until you see SQL Developer and click the link to download it. You will need an Oracle account to proceed. If you don't already have an Oracle account, you can create one for free.

Once you have downloaded the software, follow these steps to install it.

1. Unzip the downloaded file to a folder of your choice. Write down the full path to the folder.
2. Locate the **sqldeveloper.exe** file and double-click on the file icon to launch the program. The first time you run it, you will see a Start page like that in Figure D.1. Uncheck the Show on Startup box at the bottom left side of the screen if you do not wish to see it the next time you start SQL Developer.
3. For now, close the Start Page.

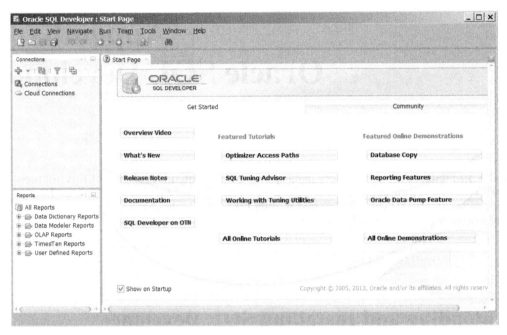

Figure D.1: SQL Developer welcome page

Creating A Connection

To work with a database from within SQL Developer, you need a connection. A connection is linked to an account. As you will use the SYSTEM account to create your own account's connection, you first need to create a connection for the SYSTEM account.

To create a connection, follow these steps.

1. Right-click the Connection folder and click **New Connection** on the popup as shown in Figure D.2.

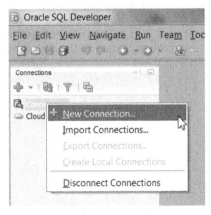

Figure D.2: Creating a connection

2. The New/Select Database Connection window will be displayed, as shown in Figure D.3. Enter a connection name and a username. The password is the password of the SYSTEM account you entered during the Oracle database installation. Check the Save Password box.

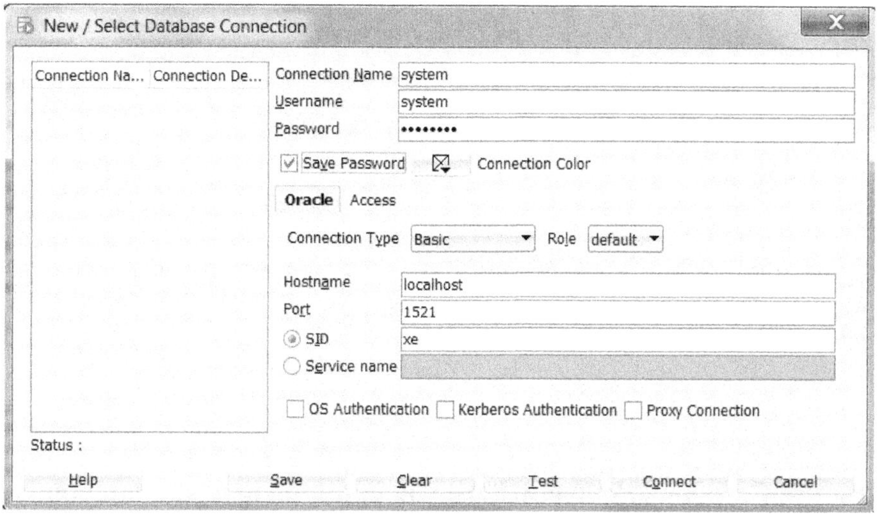

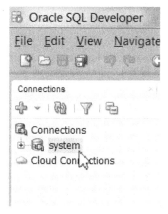

Figure D.3: The New/Select Database Connection window

3. Click the **Connect** button. The *system* connection you have just created should show up on the Connection Navigator. (See Figure D.4.)

Figure D.4: The Connection Navigator

4. Double-click on the system node to open a worksheet. The Worksheet, shown in Figure D.5, is where you type your SQL statement or source code.

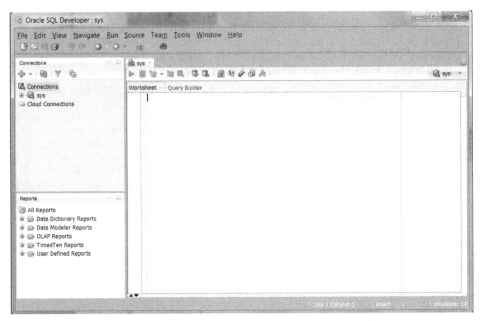

Figure D.5: A worksheet where you can type in SQL statements

Creating A Database Account

You should use your own database account (user) to try the book examples. To create a new account, follow these steps.

1. Expand the system connection and locate the Other Users folder at the bottom of the folder tree (See Figure D.6.)

Figure D.6: Other Users folder

2. Right click on it and select Create User. This is shown in Figure D.7.

Figure D.7: Selecting Create User

3. Enter a username, a password and a password confirmation, and then click the **Apply** button (See Figure D.8). When you see a pop-up window confirming that you have successfully created a user, close it.

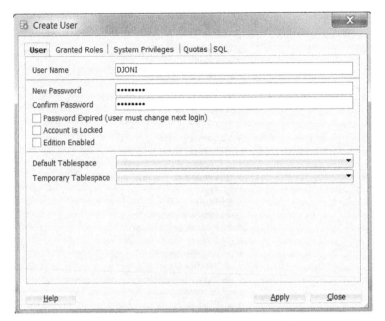

Figure D.8: Entering user details

4. On the Granted Roles tab (See Figure D.9), click the **Grant All**, **Admin All** and **Default All** buttons.
5. Click the **Apply** button and close the confirmation window and the Edit User as well.

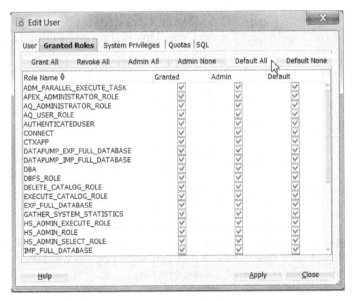

Figure D.9: Granting privileges to a user

Creating Your Connection

Using steps similar to those for creating a system connection, now you need to create a connection for your account by entering the details shown in Figure D.10.

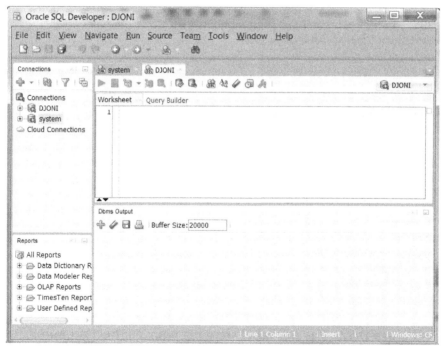

Figure D.10: Entering the details for your database connection

To create a connection, click the **Connect** button. A worksheet for your connection is opened (which is *DJONI* in my case) as shown in Figure D.11.

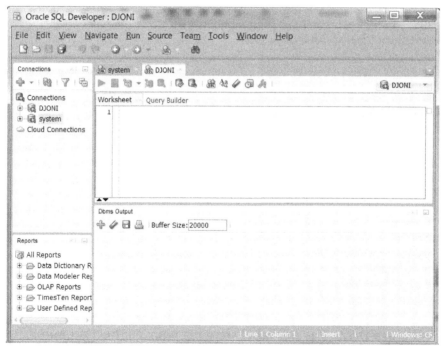

Figure D.11: The Worksheet for your connection

Showing Line Numbers

Being able to view line numbers in your code helps as error codes produced by SQL Developer often refers to line numbers. To show line numbers, click **Preferences** from the **Tools** menu, and then select **Line Gutter** and check the **Show Line Numbers** box.

Deleting the *system* Connection

Once you have a connection for your account, you do not need the *system* connection anymore and can delete it. To delete the system connection, right click on the connection node and select **Delete**. When asked if you really want to delete it, click **Yes**.

Using SQL Developer

This section shows how you can use SQL Developer to try out the book examples.

Entering An SQL statement and PL/SQL source code

To run an SQL statement, type the statement or PL/SQL code in a worksheet in SQL Developer and click the **Run Statement** button on the toolbar. If you do not see a worksheet for your connection, double-click the connection node to connect.

Note that you will see the connection name as the title of the worksheet. Figure D.12 shows a worksheet labeled DJONI.

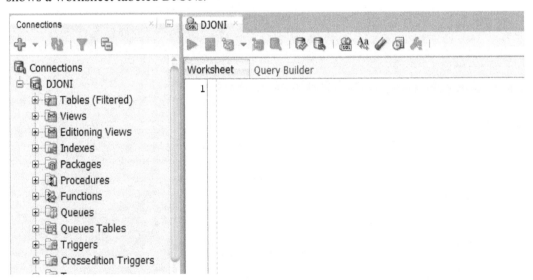

Figure D.12: The tab label showing your connection name

For example, to create the **produce** table that is used in some of the book examples, type in the SQL CREATE TABLE statement shown in Figure D.13 and click the **Run Statement** button.

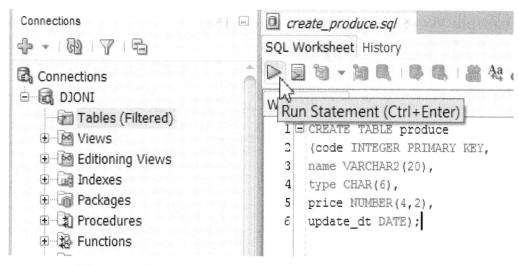

Figure D.13: Running SQL statement in the worksheet

The Script Output pane confirms that the table has been created, and you should see the **produce** table in the Connection Navigator under your connection folder (See Figure D.14). If you don't see the newly created table, click **Refresh**.

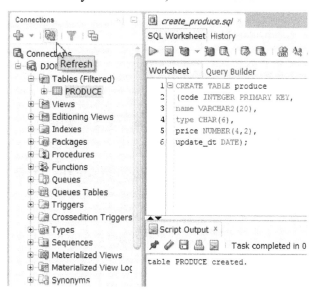

Figure D.14: Confirming a successful table creation

Inserting Rows

As an example of running multiple SQL statements in SQL Developer, copy the five statements from the **insert_produce.sql** script in Appendix A. You will need these rows when you try the book examples.

Run all statements by clicking the Run Script button or press Ctrl+Enter.

Multiple Worksheets for A Connection

Sometimes you need to have two or more programs in different worksheets. You can open more than one worksheet for a connection by right-clicking the connection and select **Open SQL Worksheet**. (See Figure D.15.)

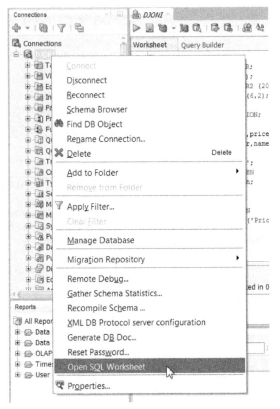

Figure D.15: Opening an extra worksheet for the same connection

Saving A Source Code

You can save a source code in a text file for later use by selecting **Save** from the **File** menu and selecting the location to save the file.

Opening a source code

You can open a source code by clicking **Open** or **Reopen** from the **File** menu and then selecting the file that contains the source code.

The source code will be opened in a new worksheet and its tab will show the name of the file.

Running SQL or PL/SQL from A File

You can execute a file that contains SQL statement or PL/SQL program without first opening the file in a worksheet as shown in Figure D.16.

Figure D.16: Executing a PL/SQL file

Clearing a Worksheet

To clear a worksheet, click its **Clear** button.

Displaying Output

Most of the examples in this book use the Oracle-supplied **dbms_output.put_line** procedure to display output. This helps as the displayed output provides instant feedback of what happens in the running program. Real-life programs might not need to display any output.

The **dbms_output.put_line** procedure has the following syntax.

```
dbms_output.put_line (parameter);
```

The parameter must be a string literal.

When the procedure is executed in SQL Developer, the string literal is displayed on the Dbms Output pane.

To see the output, before you run the example, make sure you already have a Dbms Output pane opened for the connection you are using to run the program. If you do not see the Dbms Output pane, select **Dbms Output** from the **View** menu. Figure D.17 shows the Dbms Output pane.

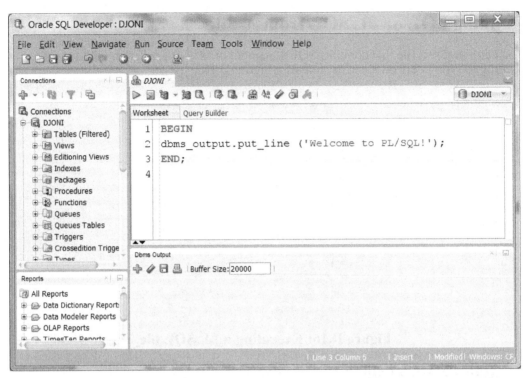

Figure D.17: The Dbms Output pane

To display an output, you need to set up the Dbms Output pane for the connection you are using to run the program. Click the + button on the Dbms Output pane like that shown in Figure D.18.

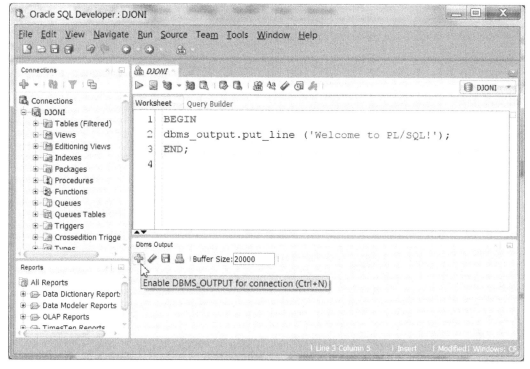

Figure D.18: Enabling Dbms Output for a connection

On the pop-up window, select the connection, and then click **OK** (See Figure D.19). As an example I select DJONI connection as this is the connection I want to use for running my PL/SQL program.

Figure D.19: Opting to show the Dbms Output

The Dbms Output now has the tab for the DJONI connection shown in Figure D20.

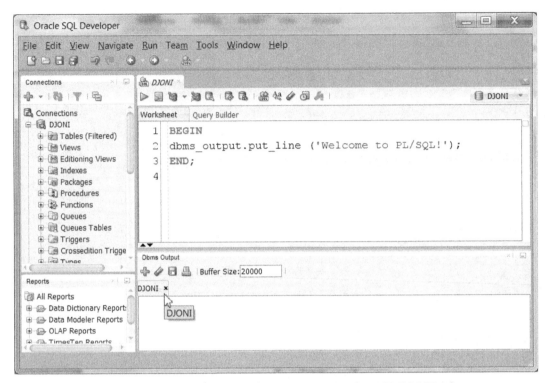

Figure D.20: The tab for the connection (DJONI)

Now, run the program by clicking the **Run Statement** button. The Dbms Output pane displays the "Welcome to PL/SQL!" greeting as shown in Figure D.21. The message on the Script Output pane shows the result of running the program. In this case, it is showing that the program was completed successfully. It would show an error message if the program encountered a problem.

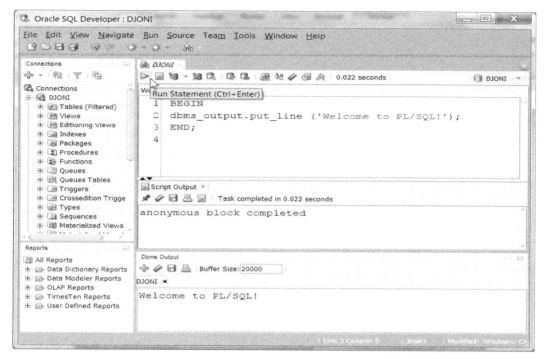

Figure D.21: The Dbms Output displaying a PL/SQL output message

Clearing the Dbms Output

To see a display output from a program, you might want to erase the output from a previous program. To clear a Dbms Output, click its **Clear** button.

Index

CPSIA information can be obtained
at www.ICGtesting.com
Printed in the USA
LVOW03s2126240516

489756LV00005B/130/P